# GREAT
## ANSWERS
### TO

# TOUGH
# CV
# PROBLEMS

In memory of Alan,
who could always recognize talent
when he saw it.

# GREAT
# ANSWERS

## TO

# TOUGH
# CV
# PROBLEMS

## CV secrets from a top career coach

## JENNY ROGERS

KoganPage

LONDON  PHILADELPHIA  NEW DELHI

First published in Great Britain and the United States in 2011 by Kogan Page Limited

| | | |
|---|---|---|
| 120 Pentonville Road | 1518 Walnut Street, Suite 1100 | 4737/23 Ansari Road |
| London N1 9JN | Philadelphia PA 19102 | Daryaganj |
| United Kingdom | USA | New Delhi 110002 |
| www.koganpage.com | | India |

ISBN       978 0 7494 6280 2
E-ISBN   978 0 7494 6281 9

**British Library Cataloguing-in-Publication Data**

A CIP record for this book is available from the British Library.

**Library of Congress Cataloging-in-Publication Data**

Rogers, Jenny.
   Great answers to tough CV problems : CV secrets from a top career coach / Jenny Rogers.
      p. cm.
   Includes bibliographical references.
   ISBN 978-0-7494-6280-2 – ISBN 978-0-7494-6281-9   1. Résumés (Employment)
2. Job hunting.   I. Title.
   HF5383.R593 2011
   650.14′2–dc22

                                                                                    2011010657

Typeset by Graphicraft Limited, Hong Kong
Printed and bound in India by Replika Press Pvt Ltd

# CONTENTS

Example CVs are available on the Kogan Page website.
To access, go to http://www.koganpage.com/editions/
great-answers-to-tough-cv-problems/9780749462802

# LIST OF CV EXAMPLES AND TEMPLATES

# INTRODUCTION

This book takes the mystery out of CV writing. It shows you how to construct a CV from scratch, starting with deciding whether the job is the right one for you, introducing you to a range of tools for creating your personal 'brand', teaching you how to use the special cryptic language of CV writing, explaining the various CV formats and when to use one rather than another, with plenty of templates and examples of how other people have solved the same problems.

It's not too hard to see why the thought of writing a CV sends so many people into a spin. If you are middle aged, how do you reduce the story of your career to two pages? If you are young with little in the way of work history, how do you eke it out to two pages? How do you write about yourself in a way that does not sound hopelessly boastful and pleased with yourself? If there is some major or minor career embarrassment in your past, how do you avoid drawing attention to it? What kind of personal information do employers want to see these days? Are there different types of CV for different professions? Do you need one at all when so much job seeking is now conducted online? No wonder then that one of the most common requests that I get as a career coach is 'Help! I've got to write a CV and I haven't a clue how to do it!'

Just as there are trends in how people are selected for jobs, so there are fashions in CV writing. But CVs are a vital part of finding a job and it's unlikely that they will ever be replaced. The internet may have revolutionized some aspects of job searching but the essential processes of matching a person to a job remain much as they have always been. The employer has a problem that they need to solve by hiring a person. Your task as a candidate is to show them how well you match up to what they need. The CV is one of the first and most vital steps. Carefully constructed, it gets the employer's attention and puts you in the frame as an interesting candidate. Your CV may appear as part of your LinkedIn page, may be the home page of your personal website, may be tinkered with by a recruitment agency on your behalf, may be e-mailed or sent in the traditional way through the post. But ultimately the means of delivery matters less than what you say and how you say it.

As a coach, I have worked with many hundreds of people on their CVs and am no longer surprised or shocked by the drafts my clients send me or the questions they ask. After all, why should people know the ins and outs of CV writing when most of us may only need to deploy a CV a few times in a career? Many of my clients have reached their early forties or older without ever having had to write one: they have been long stayers in organizations where internal promotion was decided by a tap on the shoulder or was preceded by a brief application form. A CV was unnecessary because they were already known quantities to their employers. Other clients are young and are finding it difficult to establish any kind of career in a market where young people can be particularly disadvantaged and no one has ever shown them how to write a CV. Some clients have had extended career breaks while they bring up children and then find that what they assume to be the right thing to include in a CV is no longer what is required.

## Avoiding the common traps: ten top tips

There is more about all these topics later in the book but here are my 10 top tips for avoiding all the common traps and creating the right kind of CV:

1 *Write about achievements, not responsibilities.* The most common single mistake I see on my clients' draft CVs is that these simply list their responsibilities or devote many lines to describing the organizations in which they have worked. While this is of mild interest to a future employer, it does not answer their main question: 'So what?' So what – you had those duties in theory, but what did you do in practice? So what – you did your job as laid out in your job description, but how did you add value?' Learning how to describe the ways in which you exceeded what was expected of you is one of the best ways to increase the impact of your CV.

2 *Keep it brief.* Many people know about the two-page limit in theory but in practice believe that they themselves are special cases who are allowed to sneak in extra words and pages. This is a bad idea and it also doesn't fool anybody if you reduce the margins and the type size. Once you know the special rules of CV formats and writing described in this book,

it is relatively easy to reduce the word count and keep within the two-page limit. As a double-check on length, 500–600 words is about right. Anything less may sometimes be acceptable, but anything longer is probably too long.

3 *Put the most important information on the first page.* The first page is the only one the employer will read with anything like care, so you must put your most compelling story there – and there is an art in knowing how to do this. Some people throw away this chance to make a strong first impression by littering their first page with details of their qualifications, education and training. There are some professions where this is still the right format, but it is safer to assume that in all others the middle or end of page 2 is the place for qualifications.

4 *Give the CV a pleasant, crisp, easily read layout.* We take excellent graphic design for granted in books, newspapers, TV shows and films. A CV which looks messy, fussy or difficult to read will be a loser and if it is e-mailed, the design features may disappear or reduce themselves to a nasty jumble when opened at the receiver's end. Steer clear of fancy fonts, tiny typefaces, clip art, inserted boxes and objects, photos. Stick to simple text enhancements and classic fonts with enough white space to help the eye along. This is the subject of Chapter 12.

5 *Understand that the CV is a business proposal.* The purpose of the CV is to get you on the shortlist for interview. It is the business proposition which allows you to present yourself in person later. It does not get you the job. And how you write about yourself in the CV should be totally consistent with the person the employer will meet at the interview stage.

6 *Create a strong personal 'brand'.* It can be tempting to try softening your image and to present yourself as 'safe', as in 'safe pair of hands'. Although there may indeed be some parts of your career that you should play down, the route to success in finding a job is to be positively different. That is how you will stand out from other candidates. You should invest time in identifying what you uniquely offer, as all successful brands do and which is also why their marketing departments are so powerful. I recommend that you spend time working through the material in Chapter 4 to get clear to yourself what is unique and special about you before you try writing a word of your CV.

7   *Always send a CV tailored for that job and that employer.* It is useful to have at least two CVs in different formats – for instance, chronological and skills based (Chapter 9) – on your computer for reference. But it is asking for rejection to send out a standard CV regardless of the job. Each time you send a CV it should be the result of what could be many hours of work while you carefully analyse the advertisement or job description and tailor what you say to fit what the employer wants. Never rely on the ready-made CVs that you can download from the internet: it is usually obvious where they have come from.

8   *Tell the truth.* Employers are now fully alerted to the uncomfortable fact that roughly a quarter of candidates have been shown to boost their career records to the point where the CV contains frank lies. Assume that the employer has either hired an agency that will check your claims or will make all the obvious checks (qualifications, references, dates and job titles) themselves. There is a difference between putting forward the best possible version of yourself and lying. If you lie, the chances of being found out are high – and rising all the time.

9   *Be ruthless about your internet presence.* Employers will Google an interesting candidate. Sometimes the candidate has presented themself impressively on their CV but their Facebook or Bebo page reveals a less desirable person, someone who drinks and swears a lot, blogs indiscreetly or who is guilty of banal chit-chat. It is easier to monitor anything you place about yourself on the internet in the first place than to remove compromising material later.

10  *Never rely on the CV alone to create the path to a job.* A personal approach to an employer is always better than trying to rely on paper or e-mail. The informal market in jobs is bigger and more vibrant than the market in formally advertised jobs and Chapters 2 and 3 are about how to exploit this market in a way that increases your chances of getting the job. So although the CV is an important marketing tool, its most useful role is in following up an approach that you have already made in person.

A good CV is a carefully crafted document. It combines an in-depth understanding of what the employer is looking for with a clear sense of your own personality and achievements. In writing a CV you are constantly blending these two elements. One HR director will speak for many here:

> I look at hundreds and hundreds of CVs a year. Only about two in a hundred ever convey that [the candidates] have done any meaningful research into my organization or what would be needed in the job, and only about one in ten ever gives an authentic impression of what the person is like. Far too many are obviously unaltered from one application to another and so very many sound as if they are describing the same person – same jargon, same attempts at buzz words – dull, dull, dull. When I read one that can show me straightaway that the person has understood our needs and is a unique and interesting character, that's when I perk up!

That's it. It takes time, persistence, care and skill to produce a CV like that. But it can be done – and the rest of this book is about how.

# 1

# WHAT IS A CV FOR?

The only purpose of a CV is to get you in front of a potential employer so that you can convince them in person of your qualities and skills. This may seem obvious but I meet many clients who believe that the purpose of the CV is to get them the job. Alas, this is not so. Some jobseekers also boil with indignation that they have sent out hundreds – or so they claim – of CVs and receive no acknowledgement, let alone an interview. Sending out hundreds of CVs is a sure sign of misunderstanding the whole job-seeking process. The CV is a business proposal where you are the product or service and, like any proposal, it can be turned down. No sensible business person sends out hundreds of identical proposals: they spend their time and energy on the special document that will increase their chances of getting what they want.

The CV is also a highly personal document. It represents how you want the world to see you and the whole point of it is to differentiate you from other people. This is why you should never, ever, let someone else write your CV for you, including professional CV writers who charge for the privilege. The result is usually a strangely muffled impression because, however much the CV professional tries to write using the 'voice' of the candidate, it never seems authentic. Also, the CVs that are produced by this method, and by their modern version, the free internet template, all seem to have an odd resemblance to one another. Where internet-derived CVs are concerned, employers may also have installed software to detect phrases that have been lifted wholesale from such sites. Get professional advice, by all means, and do show your CV to critical friends, especially those known to have a pedantic itch to correct other people's grammar and spelling, but don't hand the task over completely to someone else.

## From the employer's perspective: 30 seconds to make an impression

The employer is busy and preoccupied. Although hiring new staff is one of the most critical tasks any boss has, somehow many bosses manage to overlook its importance. Many managers also believe they have special gifts when it comes to choosing new people, claiming to know immediately whether someone is the right candidate or not. Naturally, this is just a fantasy because no one has magical powers of this sort and instant hiring judgements usually lead to chronic mutual disappointment later. When unemployment levels are high and there is a glut of good people, the employer can also be deluged with applications, so even where they claim good practice, the temptation to skimp on time and care can be overwhelming. Of course, you may be pleasantly surprised, but it is safer to assume when writing and sending your CV that:

- The employer is unlikely to read it as carefully as you have written it.

- Even when you actually get in front of them at an interview, the reading may have been superficial.

- The average amount of time spent on first scanning of a CV is a few seconds, perhaps 20, or if you are lucky, 30.

- You still have to write it as if it is going to be scrutinized with the utmost care.

- The employer is easily irritated by being offered irrelevant information or by the omission of the very things they want to see.

- When an employer politely says they will keep your CV 'on file', assume that this is unlikely.

When the employer is prepared to invest more time, has a properly professional HR department, and does understand the importance of making the right hiring decision, there will be a group of people assembled specifically to create a shortlist from the applications. They will have a checklist of the features they are looking for and will grade your CV according to how far it conforms to this list. There is more about this in Chapter 5. If your CV does not seem like a 90 per cent fit, it will go onto the discard pile.

Here is a verbatim quote from one HR professional, which gives a candid flavour of what it is like to be on the receiving end of CVs:

> We will have advertised in the local paper, in a professional journal and on our own website or possibly used a recruitment agency. I wait until the closing date. The prospect of having to deal with CVs makes my heart sink. I know it will be all too easy to reject the majority immediately. They will be scruffily presented, some may even be handwritten – I know this seems unlikely in this computer age, but it's not. Most applicants will not have bothered to read what we say about essential qualifications, so even if they might possibly have such qualifications, there's no way of knowing and I certainly haven't got the time to contact them personally to ask. I looked at one yesterday where we were recruiting for a chef with a particular set of qualifications and experience and one candidate applied claiming that he did the cooking at home and was therefore certain that he could do the job. This is not at all unusual. People let themselves down by not preparing carefully enough. So for instance, if we say 'Please give details of awarding body, your professional body PIN details' and so on, we mean it and if this information isn't there, it's a no. Time is always pressing and I'll have half my mind on all the other things I have to do that day. Unless it's an unusual and probably very senior job where there are likely to be only a few applicants, I'm afraid that's what happens. So if I get 100 applications/CVs, my aim is to get a long list of about 15 to look at later when I have a meeting with the manager who is recruiting. At best I'll be devoting 45 minutes to the entire task of this first look. I feel guilty about it, but only a bit, because there's so much pressure to get this and everything else done and since the recession hit, there are fewer of us than ever in the HR department but the volume of work is the same or higher.

All of this may make for bleak reading but it is better to be aware of it than unaware. It means that in drafting your CV it is critically important to know how the employer thinks. Your CV must instantly make the right kind of impact. In drafting it, your aim is to make such a good first impression that the employer puts it on the 'Read more carefully later' pile and then, when they do read it more carefully, can see that you should be shortlisted.

One size does not fit all where CVs are concerned. It is useful to have basic CVs on your computer but these should never be sent out unaltered. People think, 'I spent hours writing this, so I'll just bung it out and see what happens.' This absolutely guarantees instant rejection. It is immediately obvious to the employer that this is what you have done because there will be nothing in the CV which reflects what the employer says they are looking for. The employer thinks, 'If this person can't be bothered to take any notice of what I've said I want, why should I bother to read what they've written?' – so they don't. The annoyance that this causes will also be part of the reason that when you send a poorly constructed CV you are unlikely to get either an acknowledgement or a formal turn-down.

The purpose of the CV is to differentiate you from all the other jobseekers. It is also to show who you are, your job history and what the employer would be buying if they hire you. To do this well is not as easy as it may look. Some people believe that they can just hastily assemble a CV in minimal time. Actually it can easily take a day or more to craft the right document. The CV reflects your personal brand (Chapter 4) and will give an impression of you – whether you like it or not, or are aware of it or not. You can't *not* give an impression – your style of writing, the font you use, the way you describe yourself: they all tell more about you than you may realize. This is why it pays to get feedback from others and to expect to make many drafts before you are satisfied. Also, there are different types of CV, and each of these will take time to write. Getting these variants drafted is an excellent investment of your time. It is much better to be prepared so that if you see an advertisement or if a recruiter calls you, it will be possible to respond speedily. This is especially true if you are looking for employment at the top end of the market where a 'headhunter' – or search consultant, as they usually prefer to be called – rings you. Headhunters work at speed and expect their contacts to do the same. Dithering for a few days while you try to find the thinking and writing time to get your CV ready can mean that you lose the chance of being considered.

## Different types of CV

The type of CV you write will depend on the purpose you want it to serve, and this will depend in turn on the work you are bidding for and on other aspects of your job search:

Responding to an advertisement. Full career history CVs are the conventional response to a job advertisement. Two pages are the usual limit. Normally there will be a job and person specification and the art of writing the CV is to gut these documents, stripping them of their often overblown verbiage, to get to the essence of what the employer wants. Your CV then reflects this in how it is written and presented.

Speculative approaches to employers for full- or part-time employment may be better with one-page introductory CVs. The value of this style of CV is that it approaches the employer on their terms – it assumes they are pressed for time and shows that you appreciate this. Headhunters and recruitment agencies sometimes ask for this type of CV. You can always follow it up with a longer version if necessary.

Networking CVs are really just a variant of the covering letter. Here you are approaching a carefully targeted potential employer with a friendly, professional letter which also includes highlights of your career and tells them why they should agree to meeting you.

Specialist careers such as in medicine or universities have their own protocols, often needing much longer CVs, where you give more details of qualifications, publications or dates and details of every single job.

Freelance work: the formal CV is not usually what is required. Instead what the potential employer expects is something more like a few paragraphs of advertising copy.

The brief reference-point CV is for people who want to check you out or who might be looking for someone like you, so a personal website or your LinkedIn page may serve this purpose.

Chapter 9 describes all these different types of CV and there are some examples in Chapter 14.

As a start, you should put your effort into writing a full career history CV in chronological style (see page 111), because this is the easiest to do and the most common type that employers request. Once you have this in your computer, it becomes a useful starting point and memory jogger for all the other variants. The longer your career has been, the more easily you may forget the details of dates and job titles, so it may take you a little while to research your own career – but this will be time well spent as it will mean you can quickly adjust or restyle a variant when you need it. Having this material readily to hand will also mean that you can lift out and then tailor sections easily to slot into application forms and web-based bids for jobs.

# 2

# FINDING A JOB: WHERE CVs FIT

To make your CV work for you, it is important to understand where a CV fits into the whole process of finding a job. This chapter looks at the main ways to do effective job search, first through the so-called 'visible market', the jobs that are openly advertised, and secondly through what many people believe is far bigger, the 'invisible market', meaning the jobs that are never advertised.

## The visible jobs market

This is the market everyone knows: the jobs that are advertised in newspapers, magazines, through agencies and on the internet.

### Print

Recession and the rise of internet websites have lessened the importance of print as a source of job advertisements. However, this is still one of the places to look. If you don't already know, your initial research should answer the question: Where do employers advertise when they want to fill the kind of vacancy I'm looking for?

*Local papers*, including the free ones, are good places to find jobs with lowish salaries or for entry-level professional jobs, as these are often posts where there is a fair bit of churn. So jobs at the more junior levels in local authorities and schools or small local businesses may be advertised here. These papers are also good places to look for part-time work, as employers know that where parents of young children, for instance, do not want full-time employment, there is often an attraction in being able to get to work by walking, cycling or a quick, cheap bus journey.

*National newspapers* carry ads for more senior jobs that are harder to fill. Many of the broadsheet papers have supplements where they advertise jobs in different sectors on different days of the week. Sunday broadsheets are places to look for the most senior jobs, where ads are often placed as a back-up to headhunting. These jobs will also appear on the newspapers' websites.

*Specialist magazines* and newspapers are the most obvious first place to look for jobs which cannot be filled locally. So for instance, there are magazines for the construction, care, health, accountancy, education, food, broadcasting and hospitality sectors – and many more. If you already work in such sectors, you will undoubtedly know of these publications. Most also now have companion websites. If you wish to change sectors then it will pay you to research the sector first through looking at back copies of these magazines. You may be able to do this online, though most specialist magazines require that you register as a subscriber, not necessarily on a paying basis. Alternatively, you may be able to access these journals through a large library.

*Large organizations* will have their own recruitment departments. So if you have targeted such an employer, go to their website and click on the jobs tab. This will normally give you important information about how to apply as well as details of any current vacancies.

The CV or application form provides your entry point when you seek a job through this part of the visible jobs market. Normally there will be an invitation to download or send for a 'job pack', which will contain information about the organization and the job. Sometimes overeager candidates don't bother with this vital stage, just sending the CV off straightaway. This is not a good idea. Read the information carefully, especially the person specification. Craft your CV to match what the employer is looking for (Chapter 5). Be sensible: if the employer says certain qualifications and experience are essential, they usually mean that they are essential. It is one of the main complaints of employers that candidates waste their time, as they see it, with applications and CVs where nothing about the person is any kind of match to what the employer is looking for. Bear in mind too that where the employer asks for certain information on the CV (for instance, current salary, names of referees, full career history) it is crucial to supply it, even where it would be usual to omit such information on a standard CV.

## Recruitment agencies

Professional recruitment agencies are often a good way to short-circuit the job-searching process. There are many thousands of them, some offering jobs from very junior to very senior in every sector, some offering more narrowly targeted jobs in specific sectors or at particular levels.

*High-street recruitment agencies* have walk-in outlets as well as extensive internet sites. They have come a long way from their origins in offering humble secretarial and temping roles and often offer a full range of vacancies from unskilled manual work to professional and executive roles. These agencies are interested in volume. They are commissioned and paid for by employers, and many, although friendly and professional in how they treat individual candidates, are more interested in pleasing the employer than in taking any individual interest in you. An agency will not put you forward for a vacancy unless they feel reasonably certain that you are a strong candidate. There are also hundreds of internet-based agencies where you can apply only online.

*Job centres* are government-sponsored recruitment agencies with high-street offices. They also act as benefit screeners – on the face of it a baffling conflict of roles. By and large they deal with unskilled or more junior roles. Jobcentre Plus offices can also offer useful free services on CV drafting and interview skills.

*Search consultants (headhunters)* are the upmarket end of the recruitment agency world and are engaged to fill the most senior posts in organizations. They work through networking and by making confidential personal approaches to potential candidates, sometimes backed up by advertising. They may approach people who are not actually looking for a new job and will tend to see the task of persuading such a person to put their name forward as an enjoyable chase, hence the aptness of the headhunter label. Although, unlike the high-street recruitment agencies, this is an individually focused service, never expect a headhunter to be your personal job-search companion, as this is not their role. They find people for jobs, not jobs for people. As with all employment agencies, their loyalties lie with the employer, who pays handsomely for the privilege, typically around 30 per cent of the first year's salary when someone is successfully placed.

Headhunters like to work on the don't-call-us-we'll-call-you principle and you are always more attractive to them if you are in a job than if you are unemployed. Where you have been approached as a 'referrer' (someone who may be able to recommend a colleague for a vacancy), always make a note of the consultant's name and consider approaching them when you are in the job market yourself. Headhunters work in specialist sectors, so if you have a headhunting contact, ask them who in their firm handles the kind of vacancy you are seeking. Never send a CV in on spec: the whole headhunting process depends on personal contact. For this reason, the better you are at your own networking, the more likely it is that headhunters will get to know about you; so the more you speak at conferences, join working parties and generally see networking as a useful opportunity to create a mutual 'favour bank' where you expect to help others as much as you expect them to help you, the better it is.

## Getting the best out of professional recruiters

- Be as clear as possible about the kind of job you are looking for.

- Be honest about your reasons for making a move or being on the job market.

- Be realistic but not over-modest about your skills.

- Expect recruitment agencies to test you for some of the common skills needed for the job – for instance, keyboarding speed, fluency in a foreign language – before putting you in front of an employer.

- They will always ask you for a CV. Ask them what type of CV will help them to give you the best help – for instance, headhunters often ask for a one-page version (see page 120) at an initial meeting.

- Some agencies will want to reformat or even rewrite your CV. This is because they may not reveal the name of the employer to you at this stage and will feel that they know more about the potential job than you do. They also want to make sure that you do not approach the employer direct, thus cutting them out of their commission. For the same reason, they will often remove your contact details and name. Be wary about any rewriting. Ideally, ask to revise it yourself according to their guidelines. Always ask to see the edited version and don't allow misleading distortions to pass unchallenged. You, not the agency, are responsible for ensuring the accuracy and truth of your CV.

# The invisible market

When I have been a boss myself, my experience has conformed to the generally held view that more jobs are filled through informal contacts than through formal advertisements. So when I was a director of a consultancy, our one experience of using the formal market to find a new consultant was disastrous. Advertising through a recruitment agency, we over-persuaded a reluctant candidate to join us. After months of mutual misery and dissatisfaction, she resigned just after the agency collected their hefty fee. Contrast this to the many appointments we made, whether of freelance or full-time staff, who came to us through personal approaches or through existing contacts. The great majority of these people were excellent choices and we worked on the principle of partnership, understanding that they were choosing us as much as we were choosing them.

## *Attractions on both sides*

This is the first lesson for jobseekers: look to the invisible market first. Finding a job through the informal route is attractive to jobseekers and to employers alike. From the employer's perspective, you are far more likely to hire someone this way because it feels more natural – more like the normal process of making a relationship. Where the candidate comes to you through some kind of personal recommendation, this is also a plus because you will believe that there are fewer chances of there being something unpleasant about the person that you would discover only later. It is possible to take someone on for a short-term project first, just to see what their work is like, before you commit to a full-time permanent position. You do not have all the expense of advertising or using an agency. The agreement to offer a job feels as if it is more within your control as it often bypasses processes that many bosses find irritating, for instance those imposed by their HR professionals.

From the jobseeker's perspective it also has many advantages. The process of looking is energizing because you are taking charge of your career rather than waiting helplessly for someone else to decide that you are worth seeing. It forces you to focus. The hiring process often involves many conversations, most of them brief and friendly, so discussions with the potential employer are normally many times more relaxed than they are when an official interview or assessment process is involved, and it is more likely that the employer will get a better sense of what it would be like working with you. This is the reverse of the way it is when you are hired through the formal routes, when the relationship begins much more warily and has to be built later into something more personal. It is also more likely that if the employer likes what they see, even if they do not have a recognized vacancy, they may try to find something for you that would mean they could make use of your skills. This contrasts sharply with formal hiring processes where, if there is no one who seems 95 per cent suitable, it is usually unlikely that anyone on the interview panel will say, 'This candidate may not be wonderful at X but we could use him for Y. Let's offer him a job doing that.' Another advantage of getting a job this way is that you are not in direct competition with other candidates, so the focus of the conversations is on what you can offer rather than on how you measure up to rivals.

The majority of jobs found through the invisible market will be with small companies, and my experience is that many jobseekers get over-transfixed by large organizations, not realizing that it is small firms that dominate the economy. Looking to small companies is an advantage. A boss in a small company is more likely to be able to make a swift decision and to be flexible. This contrasts sharply with the well-meant but tediously slow recruitment processes which can bedevil large organizations.

The disadvantage – and it is a big one – is that it can feel daunting to put yourself so directly onto the job market. Taking the initiative yourself needs a lot of motivation and self-belief. You also need the willingness to accept that there will be a fair bit of rejection along the way, and the toughness to deal with it if and when it happens.

## Identifying your network

Take a large piece of paper and draw out your network as a series of ever-widening circles. Start with the immediate circle in the middle, writing down your close family and friends. In the next circle add as many of your work colleagues and acquaintances as you can. Whose business cards have you collected over the years? Go through your e-mail and phone address books and add those names in ever-widening circles according to how well you know the individuals. If you are on LinkedIn and/or Facebook, see who you know there. Check your Christmas card list. Go through all the names again: ask yourself, 'Who do those people know? Who might they be able to introduce me to?' Now highlight any of the people on your network who could be useful as ways of gaining entry to organizations which might have your sort of vacancy: normally, the more senior such people are, the better.

# Research interviews

Once you have identified useful contacts, your next task is to set up interviews to research the possibilities. This is an indirect but highly effective route to finding a job. You target people already in the field you want to enter and set up meetings which are information-gathering events with two aims: first, to help you decide whether you do actually want to work in this field or role; second, to create a safe way of introducing yourself to a potential employer. It is safe because there is no obligation on either side and therefore no potential for humiliation on yours. These interviews also help by making it easy for you to assess how likely you are to be shortlisted for any forthcoming vacancy – and of course to get early warning of any such vacancies, preparing you for applications and interviews in a way that will give you an advantage over other candidates. This method takes you straight to the heart of the hidden job market. The interviews may lead to job offers – but note that this is not their immediate purpose.

In your introductory letter or e-mail, say you will need 20 minutes max – and stick to that. Be clear about your purpose – it is to gather information from an in-house expert on what it is like working in their job, or, if they are a boss, what kind of people this person employs and what it takes to get there, *not* to ask for a job.

## Example

Ahilya is a 25-year-old Business Studies graduate with a good degree but she has been looking in vain for an appropriate permanent job for 18 months. She has decided that she wants a career in finance and has enrolled on a distance-learning course to become a qualified accountancy technician. To keep herself going, she has taken a number of poorly paid office temp jobs but badly wants to get the kind of experience which will make it easier to get something better paid in an accountancy role. She has a student loan to pay off and has become desperate about finding the right sort of job. Previously she has been applying for jobs in large organizations such as the NHS and local authorities, entirely through their HR departments or online and has drawn a complete blank, failing to land a single interview.

Her new strategy is to approach small firms and to make use of her contacts. In drawing up her network chart she is able to identify many useful contacts through her own ethnic community as well as through fellow students on her degree course.

She drafts a basic e-mail which she can flex according to the recipient. This one is to the nephew of a close friend of her father's. He is a successful entrepreneur in his thirties and runs an expanding accountancy practice in her home city. She knows from her informal research that his main clientele are small Asian-run businesses and that he specializes in personal and corporate tax.

---

To:

Cc:

Subject:

Dear Mohindra [1]

Our mutual acquaintance Ravindra Sanghera suggested I should contact you. My purpose in writing to you is that I need advice on how to progress my career and I know from Ravindra that you have several years of successful experience in the business world [2].

I was awarded a 2.1 degree in Business Studies from Liverpool John Moores University in <date [3] > and have now decided that I want a career in accountancy. I am halfway through – and very much enjoying – a self-funded AAT course with the UK Home Learning College [4] and am combining this with the kinds of temping roles which are giving me valuable experience in how offices actually run [5].

My ultimate aim is to find a job where I can grow my interest in personal and corporate tax [6] in a firm where it is important to develop close relationships with small business clients over a number of years. It would be so useful to get your advice about how to progress further. I know how busy you must be but I'm hoping we can arrange a meeting where I can ask you direct for hints and tips about what I should do next [7]. I absolutely promise not to take up more than 20 minutes of your valuable time. I live only a few miles away from your offices and can be flexible about times, including meeting early in the day if that suits you better [8]. All my contact details are below, but I will phone your office in a day or two to see if a meeting [9] is possible.

Many thanks.
Ahilya Madhavan

1  Ahilya has checked with her father's friend that it will be appropriate to address the recipient informally as he is still relatively young himself, and also that it is OK to mention her father's friend by name. Mentioning this close mutual acquaintance means that on courtesy grounds alone she is unlikely to be ignored.
2  Tells him that she has already done some research.
3  Shows she is a serious contender. Straight factual information.
4  'Self-funded' conveys determination. Doing the qualification shows she's focused.
5  Shows she's not just hanging around doing nothing, but disguises the insecurity of her current employment status.
6  Reflecting exactly the kind of business the recipient has.
7  Note that she makes it clear she is *not* asking for a job. Most people enjoy giving advice of this sort.
8  Nice touch, which acknowledges that many professional people do have unscheduled time first thing in the morning.
9  The chances are that Mohindra will e-mail back straightaway, but if he doesn't, the initiative lies with Ahilya.

The real client on whom this is based made around 12 such approaches, all to people who agreed to meet her. This was number 10. It resulted in a series of further meetings with the managing partner in this accountancy firm and the offer of an intern job for six weeks at rather low pay. This went so well that a full-time job swiftly followed. Ahilya completed her accountancy technician course, is still with the firm, and is now progressing to a more advanced accountancy qualification.

## How to handle the meeting

Dress carefully: something formal is essential. Also check how long it will take you to get there, and research the person's background – this is easier than ever now through Google and social networking sites. Remember that this is not a selling meeting: your aim is to see the world through the eyes of your interviewee.

At the meeting:

1  Restate your purpose and recheck on the amount of time your contact has available. Promise again not to exceed it and keep an eye on the clock throughout.

2  Ask how your contact got to their present position: what qualifications and experience did they have en route?

3  Ask what changes are on the horizon for the sector/job in the immediate future and what kind of person will be needed to solve any problems that will result.

4  Ask how easy or difficult it is to gain entry to the job/sector and what qualifications or experience the typical employer will be seeking.

5  Ask about the specific challenges facing this person and their organization or department.

6  Ask for two or three new names or sources of information; double-check how these people spell their names, what their job titles are and ask for their contact details. Ask permission to mention your interviewee's name when approaching these new contacts.

7  Ask whether there are any actual vacancies likely to arise in the near future and what kind of person will be needed to fill them.

8  Thank the person courteously and enthusiastically for their time.

Afterwards:

1  Write a thank-you e-mail which includes your mobile number.

2  Write up your notes.

3  Follow up the suggested contacts, mentioning the name of the person who suggested that you get in touch. If the possibility of a job has been mooted, follow it up separately – don't muddle the two processes.

Where these meetings reveal the prospect of an actual job, this is the point at which you send your CV. Note that, again, this is in sharp contrast to the way jobs are filled in the visible job market, where the CV acts as your introduction. Where the invisible job market is concerned, the CV comes later.

## Networking and speculative letters

Once you have researched the possible entry points into a company, it is often useful to write a speculative letter. As I sat down to write this section I received one of many typical e-mails:

I am an occupational psychology graduate.
Do you know of any occupational psychology opportunities?
Thank you for your help.
I hope to hear from you soon
Yours faithfully
< Name >

Everything about this communication hits the wrong note. I have never heard of the sender and she cannot even be bothered to address me by name; in fact, there is no salutation at all. There is no clue about how she has got hold of my e-mail address. Equally, there is no clue about what kind of job the sender is looking for – an 'occupational psychology opportunity' is far too vague; what kind of opportunity? What does the sender have to offer? The e-mail ends with the absurdly formal sign-off 'Yours faithfully'.

The purpose of speculative letters and e-mails is to get you in front of the potential employer in circumstances where no actual job has been advertised but you suspect that work of some kind might be available. For instance, you may know that the employer often engages people for freelance, part-time, interim or temporary project work. There is no point whatsoever in spraying letters out at random – this is a sure way to be rejected. It is far better to narrow your focus and to send out one or two well-targeted letters at a time. It would be more unusual to land a full-time job via this route, though entering as a part-time contractor is indeed an effective way of finding full-time, permanent work when you can show the employer how brilliantly useful you are.

Research is essential before you write the letter. As someone who is often on the receiving end of such communications, I am struck by how little effort the majority of my correspondents have made. Their main mistakes have been:

- Making it obvious that the letter is mass produced. My name and the company name have just been pasted in through mail merge.

- Getting the spelling of my name or the company wrong – for instance, not bothering to check whether Rogers is spelt with or without a 'd' or how I spell my first name.

- Describing their life purpose in absurdly overblown terms. Examples:

- My mission: to convert the world to coaching.

- My life purpose is to bring about a better world.

- My passion: humanity!

● Making vague requests for 'help' as in the example I quote above from the occupational psychology graduate.

● Claiming the right to address me as if we were best friends at the same time as making over-the-top claims about themselves in a way that will alienate. Here is one extract, altered slightly to spare the writer his well-deserved embarrassment.

---

Hi Jennifer [1]

Like you [2] I care passionately about the future of executive coaching and I write as an internationally acclaimed [3] executive coach and I'm betting my reputation (ouch [4]!! on you're [5] needing someone like me to get you the new clients that will transform your practise [6]. One of our professions [7]' most distinguished folk is hereby asking, nay demanding, that you see him [8]!!

Please call me to set up a meeting [9] – I'm at your service on 07<rest of number>.

---

[1]  No one has called me this since I was 15 years old, and 'Hi' is far too informal a way to address a total stranger.
[2]  Really? How do you know?
[3]  But I'm afraid I've never heard of you.
[4]  Never put slang or exclamation marks in this kind of e-mail or letter.
[5]  Grammatical error.
[6]  Wrong spelling. And how do you know I want to expand? Actually, I don't.
[7]  Apostrophe in wrong place.
[8]  Can you give me one good reason why I should?
[9]  Never leave the ball in the recipient's court.

The chances that any recipient would respond enthusiastically to such a communication are, I'm afraid, minimal.

## Tactics that work

Carry out research calls or interviews first as described earlier in this chapter and only then follow up with a letter. Part of the research conversation will be about the type of person that the employer hires or needs. Your letter or e-mail should reflect whatever this is.

Start your letter or e-mail by mentioning a name known and respected by your recipient. Obviously you must only do this if you have that person's permission. Courtesy dictates that you will get some kind of a reply, even if it is a polite turn-down. Even better, if you have met your target recipient at a conference or networking meeting and exchanged business cards, remind them how you met.

Examples:

Your colleague Simon Smith suggested that I should contact you as he felt I might be able to offer you useful skills and experience.

When we met at International Expo < date >, I promised to follow up with a brief letter outlining my experience and where I think I might be able to add value to < name of company >.

I am a friend and former colleague of Maria Silver and she has many times spoken warmly about you and < name of company >.

Be straightforward about what you are looking for. Being indirect and too clever by half doesn't fool anyone. Your reader could receive dozens of such requests a week and the one that is direct stands more chance of being taken seriously, especially if this is how it opens. Sometimes it also pays to explain why you are looking, if the reason is benign – ie without any sinister overtones such as having been sacked.

Examples:

My reason for writing: I am a highly qualified and experienced freelance IT trainer looking to expand my client portfolio. I know you work with a bank of such people and would like to set up a meeting with you to discuss what I offer.

My immediate career goal is to find a school willing to sponsor me for my teaching practice, which as you know, is a mandatory part of becoming a qualified teacher. I am hoping you could be that school.

As a result of my partner's promotion, I am relocating to the Midlands and seeking temporary or project work as an interim nurse manager. My area of special interest is Intensive Care, in which I have 10 years of continuous and successful experience. As your NHS Trust is the biggest NHS employer in the area, I am writing to you to set up a meeting to explore any opportunities there may be in your Trust.

Depending on how much you know about the target company and recipient, consider just sending the letter and following up with a proper CV when you have a better understanding of what they are actually looking for.

Address your letter or e-mail to the right person. Surveys show that up to 70 per cent of such communications are sent to the wrong person, often to the managing director or chief executive of a large company. Such people are most unlikely to agree to meet anyone other than a person at their own rarefied level. Find out who actually makes the hiring decisions in the department or company you are targeting and address your letter to that person. This may be an HR professional or a named manager. Sometimes it is worth sending two letters simultaneously, one to the HR professional and one to the departmental or unit manager, making it clear that this is what you are doing.

Never expect the recipient of your letter to make the next move: that should always lie with you. Say you will call to follow up – and do so.

The body of the letter is in other respects exactly like a covering letter for an advertised job (Chapter 11).

# 3

# CVs IN THE E-WORLD

The internet has revolutionized the whole process of researching and applying for jobs. This chapter is about how to navigate your way through the world of online advertisements, online applications and social networking sites.

## Job boards

There are thousands of sites offering jobs. These vary from the large and well known such as Fish4Jobs.co.uk and Monster.co.uk to specialist sites catering for more narrowly focused professions and interests. There are also sites which are the present-day equivalent of classified ads, and which include job ads along with ads for second-hand sofas and computers. Gumtree.com, for instance, often seems to have slightly quirky and offbeat jobs, many of them part-time or temporary for people whose careers may not have taken conventional paths. Gumtree also has city-specific sites.

These sites are free to job applicants and make money from the employers who pay to post their vacancies online. They can be useful when you are a jobseeker, offering a range of services such as:

- advice on writing CVs and covering letters;
- alerting you to jobs which match your career goals;
- enabling you to apply online for vacancies;
- the chance to browse thousands of jobs, giving you a quick and accurate idea of salary range, job descriptions and the availability of employment in your geographical or interest areas;
- telling you how many other people have already applied for any particular job.

Where you are searching for a job, use your favourite search engine and enter the key words. For instance, if you are a senior teacher looking for promotion to a deputy headship, enter 'teacher deputy head jobs'. When I did this my search immediately brought up eight directly relevant sites and I could have refined the search even more by naming a city or area.

All of this is useful and people do find jobs this way. If the experience of my own clients is anything to go by, the more specialist the site, the more likely it is to produce an attainable job. It seems more dubious that it can all work the other way around – that is, posting your CV online so that potential employers can find you. I have worked with many dozens of clients who have uploaded their CVs only to find that it is utterly one-way traffic and no employer has ever approached them as a result of their effort.

Some applicants suspect that with less reputable or less successful sites, some especially juicy jobs are advertised in order to boost the site's treasury of CVs – but that no such job has ever truly existed. So if a job seems too good to be true – for instance, a high salary for what seems like a suspiciously small number of duties or minimal qualifications – then it probably is.

It is possible that these sites have been too successful for their own good. Making an application is quick and easy since many of the sites just ask you to attach an existing CV. Employers can thus be bombarded with hundreds, sometimes thousands, of applications from people who think they may as well give it a go, despite having no real interest in the job. In the earlier days of these sites, employers were probably initially pleased with the number of applications they got, but several then found that there were so many of the darned things that they had to employ more staff just to deal with the numbers. This meant they were spending money rather than saving it, thus defeating the original purpose.

Online CVs seem to work best for jobs where some degree of standardization can be assumed – for instance, entry- or middle-level jobs in teaching, nursing and office administration. They work far less well for more senior jobs or ones where you need to demonstrate attitudes, skills and achievements. So you could let an employer know that you are a registered general nurse with three years of experience at staff nurse level and with specialist orthopaedic knowledge. Whether you can convince them of your so-called 'soft skills', for instance, your ability to offer sensitive care to patients, will depend on how convincingly you write as well as on how clearly the employer signposts the evidence they want to see.

If you do post your CV online, you need to absorb and then carefully follow the instructions on the site about how to submit it. This will usually involve using plain text of some kind and avoiding fancy graphics. Sometimes even bullet points are debarred.

# Other online opportunities

Recruitment agencies combine walk-in offices with large online sites. The advantage they have over internet-only sites is that there is often an actual human being whose name is given on the advertisement and a telephone number to call plus a locally available actual place in which to double-check the job. Agencies put minimal information online, so to make an impressive application you do ideally need the further information that a live human can supply. Similarly, most specialist journals offer job advertisements where you can apply online or use the online facility to download more information about the job.

Large employers also have pages on their websites where they advertise vacancies. So if you are interested in, for instance, seeing whether your local hospital or local council might have jobs, you should go to their website, click on the vacancies page and follow the instructions for applying. Normally there will be a named person who can be phoned. If so, always take advantage of this offer.

## Pre-screening

To guard against hundreds of inappropriate applications, agencies and large employers are increasingly making successful pre-screening a condition of going any further with your application. This screening may be something as simple as four questions with yes/no boxes for the answers – such as:

- Do you earn between £20,000 and £30,000 in your current job?

- Have you worked for an energy company previously?

- Do you have a first class or 2.1 Honours degree?

- Are you legally entitled to work in the UK?

Unless you can answer yes to all four questions you will be unable to go further. Note that answering yes when the real answer is no will merely annoy the employer when they discover the truth.

It is also increasingly common to subject applicants to more elaborate screening. This may consist of a personality questionnaire, often of a rather simple sort, designed to eliminate people who seem to have obvious personality flaws. Alternatively there may be ability or aptitude tests which have to be completed under time pressure. As an example, one company which sells such tests to employers has an entry-level test for unskilled jobs, which asks the candidate to read a clock face accurately, do some simple arithmetic and answer comprehension questions which also function as a reading-ability test. Other tests offer employers the chance to assess aptitude for sales, healthcare, office, mechanical and service jobs, among many others. Pre-screening of qualifications, credit and work status and driving licence is also available via software sold to employers. Normally you have to give your consent before submitting to this scrutiny.

It is now common to see pop-up advertisements from companies offering to place your CV on their sites for a fee. Such companies may also sell services such as advice on writing CVs, CV templates, books, workshops and coaching. The additional services may be useful, but essentially you do not need to pay to have your CV put online when there are so many reputable agencies who will do it for free. Some of these purported agencies are unfortunately fronts for identity theft, extracting sensitive personal information such as your bank and national insurance details from you in the guise of putting you forward for a job. Never, ever, disclose such information to an agency (see also page 70). If you are asked for it at the application stage, it is a sure sign of fraud.

## Video

Some agencies and sites will suggest that you post a brief video of yourself and of course technology makes it easy to do so – easy, that is, to make the actual recording. I recommend great caution here. I worked for many years as a BBC TV producer and observed that although some people can eventually learn how to talk to a camera confidently and as if they are addressing a friend, few can do so without a great deal of feedback and training. What is much more likely is coy simpering, much hesitating, drying up and giggling or the wooden, robotic performance which suggests that you have learnt your lines but have no idea how to deliver them unaffectedly and with feeling. None of this will do you the slightest good with an employer, so unless you are one of those rare people with natural aptitude, I suggest you skip the video.

## Keywords

Assuming you get past the pre-screening stage, employers have invested in software which scans CVs for keywords. There is no great mystery about these – they will be the words included in the job description. Using these words is important whether you are making an electronic or a traditional application. Be aware that when the application is electronic and the employer is using keyword software, creative interpretations of the words the employer uses will lead to your CV being rejected. So if the employer calls the job Customer Relations Manager, it would be dangerous to refer to it as Client Liaison Manager. Use the exact words in the person specification or job description. Other keywords for which the software will search include the names of specific qualifications, competencies (see page 67), plus experience and technical terms used in your sector or profession. There may be elite employers that the hiring organization is looking for in your background – for instance, one of the large consultancies, media or accountancy companies. If you have such experience, always mention the employer. Tick any box that specifies location; leaving it blank may suggest that you are reluctant to move. Other phrases that the software will be designed to pick up might include length of experience in years. Make sure that when you can satisfy such criteria, this appears in your CV. Never leave any box blank as it may lead to instant rejection.

Watchfulness is necessary in sending or posting your CV electronically and despite any care you take, you may find yourself helpless in the hands of others. Even when you are applying for a job through a reputable route, your CV can end up in places that can embarrass you. A senior client of mine was struggling to dismiss a poorly performing team member who promptly went off sick, claiming he was suffering from 'stress' and 'depression', was too ill to work, and was signed off by his doctor for several months. Within a few days my client received via e-mail a copy of this individual's application for a job at a competitor organization. He had ill-advisedly given my client's name as referee without her consent and the prospective new organization had by mistake sent her a copy of his application – in which he claimed to be in robust health and also described his current organization as 'dysfunctional'. Not only did this character not get the job for which he was applying but his fragile hold on his existing job was greatly weakened. Another client found that in her quest for promotion through a job site, her CV somehow found its way back to her current employer. You may be able to blank out details of current employment to prevent this happening and there should be advice on the site about how to do this if you wish to guard your anonymity.

## Social networking sites

It's impossible to overemphasize the importance of the need for caution in the electronic world. Once information about you is out there in cyberspace, it's virtually impossible to stop it being widely available. Two high-profile cases make the point. In 2010, Paul Chambers, a 27-year-old trainee accountant, was prevented by heavy snow from flying to meet a woman he had encountered online. He tweeted the following message: 'Crap! Robin Hood Airport is closed. You've got a week and a bit to get your shit together otherwise I'm blowing the airport sky high!!' Mr Chambers was surprised to find himself interrogated for eight hours by police, was subsequently convicted of causing a menace under the Communications Act of 2003, lost his job and was fined £1,000 plus prosecution costs. The US stand-up comedian Joe Lipari used his Facebook page to threaten to shoot staff at the Apple store on Fifth Avenue after they had failed to sort out a problem with his iPhone. He was charged with making terrorist threats, something he claimed to find hilarious, since, like Mr Chapman, he thought it crashingly clear that he was only joking. As I was writing this, my e-mail pinged to tell me I had a message from Facebook. Along with the message was a link to other 'friends' I might know, including a female acquaintance from many years back whom I'll call Sonia. When I clicked on her profile it told me that her interest was 'relationships' and that her hobby was 'men, one-night stands and sex'. Sonia's photograph showed her doing what looked like pole-dancing in an extremely skimpy outfit that might have seemed OK on someone 30 years younger. For a few further clicks, a string of chatter was also available containing multiple swearwords, accounts of drunken nights and indiscreet gossip. For all three of these people, it's entirely probable that what they posted was meant ironically or as an obvious joke. For instance, Paul Chambers's barrister reminded the Court of Appeal that the three exclamation marks in his tweet surely indicated that his remarks were not meant to be taken seriously. The trouble with any written communication is that irony and joking are not at all easy to identify and adding exclamation marks definitely does not make it plain to a reader what your intention is or your frame of mind when writing it.

All of this matters a lot because if an employer is interested in you as a candidate, they will be highly likely to search your name on the internet. This could take them straight to any social networking sites on which you appear. If my former acquaintance, Sonia, were looking for work, what impression would her Facebook page give? Undoubtedly it would be of a woman with loose sexual morals foolishly trying to seem younger than she is, given to swearing a lot, interested in sex and not much else – however unfair and one-dimensional this is compared with the real person, whom I remember quite differently.

You should also look at what your friendship or colleague network says about you on such sites. Do these friends give the right impression? How do they reflect on you?

It may seem harsh, but if you insist on appearing on Facebook or MySpace and also are addicted to tweeting, then you might want to stick to the most bland and simple information. Even if there is nothing scandalous or overtly naughty in your online chatting, so much of such exchanges is unguarded. Frankly, if you are not one of the friends so addressed, it can look like vacuous and trivial yapping – not the kind of thing to impress an employer with your professionalism. Most of the people who post this material probably believe that they are merely talking privately to trusted friends, but the confidentiality the sites provide is the frailest of defences against intrusion. If you do have a trail of these indiscretions and might want to delete your account when you are job searching, this can prove more of a struggle and take longer than you might imagine.

As social networking sites have grown, so has the number of people who become seriously addicted to them, sometimes spending many hours a day in chatter with online friends. Beware of seeming as if this is how you spend your time: any employer will conclude that networking rather than working is your real interest.

Although sites like Twitter do seem to specialize in the inane, they can also be used for a serious purpose. An article in the *Guardian* newspaper (20 February 2010) described how a final-year student in Australia sent out a tweet saying 'I want an internship with a leading social media agency or leading online PR firm in Syd. Anybody have any suggestions or recommendations?' This led to a response from a senior account manager at Ogilvy PR in Australia who eventually did offer her an internship which has turned into a permanent job.

# Professional sites

Professional network sites are a rather different matter. LinkedIn has become powerful in a few short years but there are thousands of other sites appealing to specialist interests, many of them hosted by serious and totally respectable professional associations and interest groups. The sites are lucrative because they have so much potential for advertising. In fact, the more the network is an obvious and large niche market, the more attractive it can be to advertisers. Such networks are also places where employers might look or be contacted about vacancies.

Don't be misled by the informal, friendly feel these sites have. When they offer you the chance to upload your CV you should make it as professional as you can, using the one-page CV format as your guide (see page 120). Sites such as LinkedIn also give you opportunities to mention people who recommend you. If you have no recommendations, consider approaching people direct to ask for them. A fellow coach and facilitator has taken full advantage of this:

> I have several links on my LinkedIn page to clients who have been enthusiastic about my services and generously agreed to give me recommendations after I'd approached them. I chose them carefully to match the kind of work I really enjoy doing – in other words being specific about my particular niche in the market: managing stress/work overload and my track record with senior managers in the hospitality sector. For minimal effort I have acquired several new client organizations who approached me in the first instance direct from LinkedIn.

Make sure that your photograph is flattering, recent, has high-level definition and that ideally it has been professionally taken. This is not the place for a blurry picture of you with your sweet five-year-old twins or for a honeymoon snap where you are raising a glass to your adorable spouse. It should be a pleasant head and shoulders photograph where it is clear that you are wearing the business dress customary in the world where you are seeking a job.

Keywords matter here too, so make sure your CV uses the words that are common in the sector in which you want to work and for the kind of role you want. This will make it easier for potential employers to find you. Some of the sites have a box you can tick indicating that you might be open to job offers. Where the sites have a chat/debate/discussion forum, join in, as this, again, will raise your profile. Most sites also have an 'Any answers?' forum, so taking part in this will allow you to demonstrate your expertise.

LinkedIn, like Facebook, suggests who else you might know through networks and people you have in common. You can also allow the site to search your e-mail inbox to find people you already know who have an existing profile. Where you see that one of these people could be in the hiring business, you can contact them through the site, typically asking for advice about vacancies or about what is involved in recruitment, using the social networking site as yet another way to do a research interview (see page 19) and as an introduction to a face-to-face meeting. As with every other kind of networking, it's about finding people who can help you and building a relationship with them rather than hoping to find a job directly. It can also pay immediate dividends to ask everyone in your network to accept an invitation from you, as this coaching client of mine did:

> When I drafted my personal network on paper first as you
> suggested, I realized how many people I knew and also realized
> how powerful it could be to invite them all through LinkedIn.
> Some already had profiles, some ignored me but most accepted
> straightaway and, of course, this immediately gave me dozens of
> their contacts. I combed them all and selected several as targets.
> This is how I found an interim role as a manager and I'm pleased
> to say it has led to several others and now I am firmly on track for
> a long-term interim career. I update my page constantly, have a link
> to my personal website and whenever I meet someone new, I send
> them an invite. These networks are the way of the future for me!

Don't spread yourself too thin with online social networks, otherwise you will spend all your time updating and contributing. Probably three is the maximum, one of them a general-interest site such as LinkedIn and two for contrasting specialist interests. Online methods are not the solution to all job-seeking problems but I do recommend that you add them to the traditional routes such as face-to-face networking, agencies and classified advertisements.

# 4

# YOU THE BRAND

To write a powerful and convincing CV, you have to be clear what you are selling. It can be uncomfortable to consider yourself in this way – in other words, that you are a product – but if you fail to think carefully about who you really are, what you want and what you offer an employer, you will reduce the chances of writing the kind of CV that gets the employer's attention. This chapter is about how to identify and then convey your personal brand, one of the foundations of a successful CV.

## Why your personal brand matters

One mistake that some jobseekers make is to try selling themselves to an employer as all-round, all-purpose, all-wonderful employees. The effect is to produce a smudged and insipid picture which the employer has no difficulty in discarding. The solution is to be more focused, not just in how you search but in what you convey about yourself – and this starts with thinking about your personal brand.

A successful brand is one that clearly sets itself apart from its competitors, and this is what you have to do when you write a CV. There is no successful brand in the world that pretends to be able to solve every problem: all of them aim to differentiate themselves. When a brand fails, one of the most common reasons is that it does not distinguish itself from its competitors, or that people simply don't know what it offers. The best recent example is the failure of Woolworths as a retailer in the UK. In its last few years it was impossible to be certain what you would find in the stores other than pick 'n' mix sweets, toys, CDs and video products. Could you be certain of finding a reel of cotton there? Or stationery? Or a garden hose? The promise of the original chain, to sell cut-price everyday items that any household could need, was blurred by many years of management dithering and ineffectual change as well as by the activity of so many competitors. The near-collapse of Marks & Spencer in the late 1990s was another example of a company where it became difficult to see at a glance who they envisaged as their customer – it seemed to be Mr and Ms Anyone and therefore appealed to no one. Contrast this with successful brands where it is completely clear who the customer is and what you can expect to find in the shops – for instance, Claire's Accessories sells pocket-money trinkets for little girls; the Pret A Manger sandwich chain sells upmarket snacks at premium prices and appeals to people in a hurry who also like the promise of natural ingredients freshly assembled every day and don't mind paying more for the privilege. A successful brand also makes it clear who is *not* a customer, so the Pret customer is most unlikely to buy a sandwich from Subway – on the face of it a competitor, but in practice not, because the Subway customer wants much cheaper, simpler food.

Successful people are also brands. So everyone's favourite leader, Sir Richard Branson, is instantly associated with informality, risky adventures with balloons and entrepreneurial cheek. Katie Price is known for her Page Three posing, vulnerability and down-to-earth sexiness. The personal brand of celebrities can also change, so Victoria Beckham, known originally as a pop singer in a girl band, then as the too-thin wife of a famous footballer, is now more associated with the expensive and beautiful dresses she designs. These people make the point that a successful personal brand is never about perfection. Richard Branson's scruffiness is legendary, Katie Price has never concealed the fact that her enormous breasts are the result of surgery rather than a freak of nature; Victoria Beckham has allowed documentary films to be made where her over-concern with appearance has been clear for all to see. Brand is also about authenticity, being yourself – but the best possible version of yourself. Knowing what this is will allow you to write the CV that means you stand out from competitors rather than making the mistake of wanting to seem just like them.

In practice we are all communicating our personal brand all the time, whether we are aware of it or not. So choosing one garment rather than another to put on in the morning is a brand choice. How you speak and what you say, how you are with colleagues and family, the way you write an e-mail or communicate on Twitter – these are all expression of brand.

## Discovering your brand

Here are five exercises to help you discover your brand.

### Exercise 1: your self-image

When you think about yourself at your best, what words or phrases do you use to describe yourself? What would you like people to say about you?

### Exercise 2: feedback from others

Now you need to check this out with others. Yes, this can be embarrassing because it asks you to go beyond normal British politeness, but it is a highly revealing exercise. The simplest and most direct way to find out what others think about us is to ask them. One reason we don't do this is fear of what we might hear – but others hold views about us whether we know such views or not, and learning what these are is vital to self-development. Also, there is always far more that is positive than we might believe.

The second reason is lack of skill in asking the questions.

Select six people who know you well. At least one of them should be someone more senior than you. E-mail or call them to fix a time to talk, saying that you are on a mission to collect feedback on yourself. Reassure them that it will take 10 minutes – no more. Don't bottle out by agreeing to an e-mail version – it is vital to actually ask the questions. Arm yourself with a notepad and pen for the actual interviews.

## The questions

Say:

> I'm collecting feedback as part of my preparation to get my CV together. I'm really interested in your views on me and I'm going to be talking to five other people as well.
>
> Question 1. In living/working with me, what do you see as my strengths?

Most people will give vague headline-style replies. This is because they are not sure how direct or candid they can be. An example might be:

> Well, you're very good at motivating your team.

This does not count as feedback – it's far too vague. You then need to probe:

> When you say I'm good at motivating, could you tell me a bit more?

Or:

> Could you give me an example of where you've seen me do this?

Write down *everything* your feedback giver says, without adding any comments of your own except 'Thank you.'

Now say that you are going to turn to your less strong areas.

> Question 2. What would you say I'm less good at, in your view?

People may be even more hesitant here, so you need to be able to reassure them that you really want to know. Use the same techniques of asking for specifics, and probing generalizations or vague statements.

Question 3. What would your advice be to me about how to market myself for a job?

It's really important to avoid any defending or explaining. Just nod, smile, write it all down and once more say 'Thank you.'

Just because people hold a view of you does not make it 'true' or the last word about you. Equally, perceptions may need to be managed. Feedback is not an instruction to change, but it is virtually always a thought-provoking process and can be a vital platform for understanding what your personal brand is and how to project it.

The ability to gather and listen to feedback is a rare skill – and just doing it is a sign of a mature human being who is grown-up enough not to be defensive and to be open to what others think. These qualities are attractive to employers.

## Exercise 3: your personality

You may already have taken various well-known personality question-naires such as the Myers–Briggs Type Indicator®, the Occupational Personality Questionnaire (OPQ)® or the Belbin Self-Perception Inventory©. If so, you will already have benefited from the useful insights that such questionnaires can provide. It is also possible to take free versions of something like these questionnaires on the internet (the originals are normally only available to trained and licensed practitioners). The questionnaire that follows is a short version reflect-ing many of the factors that such questionnaires assess. How would you describe yourself? There are no rights or wrongs here: any of these 'ways to be' has its own strengths and weaknesses. For instance, if you like your own company more than you enjoy seeking out others, then you could be over-solitary or just a quiet person who is a good listener and can do their best work when alone. If your preference is to seek out others, then you may be a socially confident person or, if you overdo it, a restless and unsettling presence. Which description in the following list is more like you? Highlight or tick one in each pair. If you are unsure, then mark one of the middle boxes, whichever seems nearest to how you see yourself. But note that there is no actual middle score. This is deliberate: you must choose one side or the other.

| WHICH IS MORE LIKE YOU? | | | | | |
|---|---|---|---|---|---|
| Like my own company | | | | | Seek out others |
| Concrete thinking, practical, like facts | | | | | Abstract thinking: like theories and ideas |
| Like excitement, risk | | | | | Like predictability, security |
| Detail conscious | | | | | Big-picture focus |
| Talking | | | | | Listening |
| Put others first | | | | | Being assertive |
| Serious, calm | | | | | Fun seeking, lively |
| Optimistic – see the positives | | | | | Cautious: see the problems |
| Seek change | | | | | Like tradition |
| Shy, reticent, modest | | | | | Flamboyant, like attention |
| Prefer to be the leader | | | | | Prefer to be the follower |
| Trusting of others | | | | | Guarded with others |
| Private | | | | | Readily talk about myself |
| Self-sufficient | | | | | Team player |
| Stressed | | | | | Relaxed |
| Like to have rules for guidance | | | | | Like to make it up as I go along |
| Down to earth | | | | | Imaginative |
| Feelings always visible | | | | | Hide my feelings |
| Conscientious | | | | | Bend the rules |
| Innovative | | | | | Respect established ideas |
| Like to plan | | | | | Like to stay flexible |

What picture emerges for you here? Write down the key words.

| | | | |
|---|---|---|---|
| | | | |
| | | | |
| | | | |
| | | | |

## Exercise 4: thinking about intelligence

Traditionally, the only intelligence that mattered was IQ – intelligence quotient, the tests developed for, among other purposes, selecting children at age 11 for grammar or secondary modern schools in the early–mid 20th century. Among many problems with the original IQ tests were that they often depended on general knowledge and therefore favoured the better off and already well educated, and did not discriminate carefully enough between what could be achieved at 11 and what might be achieved later. Improved IQ tests are now available which get around most of these problems and are normally presented as verbal reasoning, spatial reasoning or numerical reasoning tests.

However, Professor Howard Gardner has argued persuasively that there are multiple intelligences, not just IQ. Daniel Goleman's work on EQ – emotional intelligence – is also well known. Understanding what your 'primary intelligences' are is a useful way of understanding how to find a job that plays to your strengths and to represent yourself skilfully on your CV.

Which of the following intelligences are yours?

### Logic and mathematical intelligence

Liking numbers; can remember dates easily; enjoying puzzles and games such as chess; quick at mental arithmetic; liking to work out mathematical formulae; believing in the importance of scientific experiment and basing a decision on evidence. Tackling problems in a logical manner; orderly – find it easy to prioritize.

Typically held by: scientists, researchers, lawyers, mathematicians, scientists, engineers, computer experts, accountants, statisticians, researchers, analysts, traders, bankers, bookmakers, insurance brokers, negotiators, dealmakers, troubleshooters.

## Linguistic intelligence

Loving words and fascinated by where they come from and how people use them; wide vocabulary; liking to read; liking to write for its own sake, not just as a task; verbally quick and fluent; able to think on your feet; good storyteller; enjoying story-based entertainment such as film and TV serials; enjoying word games such as Scrabble or crosswords.

Typically held by: writers, journalists, poets, speakers, barristers, actors, preachers, copywriters, editors, media presenters.

## Bodily intelligence

Feeling a sense of ease in using your body; enjoying most sport as participant rather than as spectator; aware of how your body works; like being active most of the time; prefer being outdoors to indoors and working with your hands rather than with ideas; like making things where there is a tangible result; graceful and physically coordinated.

Typically held by: craftspeople, sportspeople, skilled repairers of all sorts, farmers and other outdoor workers, dancers, demonstrators, actors, athletes, divers, soldiers, firefighters, performance artists, ergonomists, osteopaths, fishermen, drivers, gardeners, chefs, acupuncturists, healers, adventurers.

## Visual-spatial intelligence

Strong sense of graphic design and acute visual awareness; interested in how rooms and buildings look and feel; at ease with plans and drawings; love to sketch, paint or draw cartoons; interested in film, fashion, clothing and other visual arts; like to push boundaries in own work; willing to spend time on getting visual details just right.

Typically held by: designers, painters, producers, artists, designers, cartoonists, storyboarders, architects, photographers, sculptors, town planners, visionaries, inventors, engineers, beauty consultants.

## Musical intelligence

Acutely aware of music in all its forms; love to sing or play, may also love to dance; may have perfect pitch and will for certain be able to hear when an instrument or voice is out of tune; may enjoy composition; keen to improve own performance in chosen instrument; take delight in concerts whether in person or in recorded form; reliable sense of rhythm and beat.

Typically held by: composers, members of choirs, singers, professional musicians of all sorts from schoolteachers to orchestral and solo performers, dancers.

## Interpersonal intelligence

Can create easy rapport with others and enjoy their company; acutely alert to small changes in demeanour of others and can adapt accordingly; psychologically curious about people; reliable intuition; often sought by others because of being 'a good listener'; able to listen without prescribing solutions; can accept wide range of behaviours from others without judging; wide circle of close friends.

Typically held by: educators, therapists, coaches, counsellors, carers, clinicians, salespeople, politicians, psychologists, clergy, actors, managers.

## Intrapersonal intelligence

Realistic self-awareness and lifelong interest in own learning and development; may be interested in formal forms of spirituality such as traditional religions or may have more wide-ranging sense of spirituality generally; like to spend at least some time in own company and will protect privacy fiercely; prefer to think independently than to be dependent on others; reflective style does not spare self from criticism.

This intelligence, like interpersonal intelligence, above, has strong connections with EQ (emotional intelligence) and its foundation quality of self-awareness.

Other 'intelligences' have been suggested – eg spiritual intelligence and moral intelligence.

There is no better-than or worse-than intelligence nor any way of diagnosing at what level we hold them. Some people may compensate for lack of opportunity to use their favourite intelligences at work by devoting a great deal of leisure time and energy to them. It is likely that traditional ways of assessing intelligence such as the IQ version are narrow and that the world needs people with a mix of all intelligences. It's also likely that we develop skill in our preferred/primary intelligences and that no one is good at all seven.

Which are your own top three?

| |
|---|
| 1. |
| 2. |
| 3. |

How far have they been reflected in your career so far?

| |
|---|
| 1. |
| 2. |
| 3. |

What influence do they need to have on your future choices?

| |
|---|
| 1. |
| 2. |
| 3. |

## Exercise 5: John Holland's career types

John Holland was a research psychologist who developed a theory that careers had their own 'personalities', strongly associated with six different types of people, each with their own preferred work environment. There may be two or even three of these brief profiles which seem to describe you to some extent, so that when you combine them they give a rich picture of the kind of work and work environment in which you will thrive and will also indicate the ones where you would be unhappy and feel like a misfit.

### Realistic: people who work with their hands

Realists are doers, people who like to make, repair, and work hands-on with tools, equipment, plants, animals or machinery, living in the here and now and not worrying too much about the future or about things which are intangible.

Put a tick in the box nearest to how far *realist* describes you.

| Very accurately | | | | | Not at all |
|---|---|---|---|---|---|
| | | | | | |

### Investigative: thinkers

Thinkers love puzzles and problem solving. They bring a meticulous, precise, scientific slant to everything they do and often have mathematical gifts. Generally speaking, they prefer to work with ideas rather than with people or objects. They enjoy academic work.

Put a tick in the box nearest to how far *thinker* describes you.

| Very accurately | | | | | Not at all |
|---|---|---|---|---|---|
| | | | | | |

### Artistic: creators

Creators value all forms of artistic expression – for instance, painting, music, textile crafts, drama, singing or writing. Even if they do not consider themselves to possess original creative talent, they value the work of people who do have gifts in these areas. Creators do not want to be like everyone else; they prize autonomy and independence.

Put a tick in the box nearest to how far *creator* describes you.

| Very accurately | | | | | Not at all |
|---|---|---|---|---|---|
| | | | | | |

## Social: the helpers

These people enjoy any activity that involves nurturing, whether it is a practical activity such as nursing and teaching or something more intangible like counselling and coaching. They feel strong emotional bonds to others, value harmony, dislike conflict and want to be valued for their social skills.

Put a tick in the box nearest to how far *helper* describes you.

| Very accurately | | | | | Not at all |
|---|---|---|---|---|---|
| | | | | | |

## Enterprising: entrepreneurs

Entrepreneurs love leadership, selling and persuading. They are happy to sell services, products or ideas. Often vivid, personable and persuasive, they have energy and ambition and are often drawn to managerial or political roles.

Put a tick in the box nearest to how far *entrepreneur* describes you.

| Very accurately | | | | | Not at all |
|---|---|---|---|---|---|
| | | | | | |

## Conventional: implementers

Implementers like to feel there is a solid framework around them in which they can plan and therefore know what to expect. They enjoy detail and routine, and value qualities such as punctuality and carefulness.

Put a tick in the box nearest to how far *implementer* describes you.

| Very accurately | | | | | Not at all |
|---|---|---|---|---|---|
| | | | | | |

# Putting it all together

From these five different approaches to identifying your brand, write down all the words which you now feel describe you, concentrating on your strengths and ignoring any weaknesses which might have emerged. The weaknesses are normally just the flipside of a strength, so someone who is good at big-picture thinking is often nothing like so good at detail. Your weakness with detail has no place on your CV, but your strength with big-picture thinking could very possibly match the employer's need to have someone in their team who is good at strategic thinking. You should end up with a collection of words which feels unique to you – a collection that could not possibly describe an all-purpose, bland candidate for a job.

| Self-image | Feedback from others | Personality | Intelligence | Career type |
|---|---|---|---|---|
| | | | | |

# Brand promise

A brand promise is what you pledge to deliver to a customer. So if an organization is a budget hotel chain, its brand promise might be to deliver affordable, clean, simple accommodation with no expensive frills. If the organization is at the other end of the hotel market, its brand promise might be to deliver a luxurious experience which pampers the customer. In CV terms, your brand promise is what you can guarantee to deliver to any employer. Brand promise is also similar to another idea borrowed from marketing: brand essence, the qualities and values you would never compromise.

Here is how two candidates defined themselves, their brand promise and brand essence. First is Sarah, a TV researcher:

> I am a thoughtful, careful, confident person who works well with routine and systems. I pride myself on accuracy and on the quality of my research. I am persistent, hard-working, conscientious, and don't give up easily. My fact checking is impeccable and I have excellent IT skills including knowing how to squeeze the best out of the internet. I am also a popular team member, committed to contributing to my colleagues' success, and my friendly telephone manner means I get on good terms with people of all types quickly, getting good stories out of them with ease.
>
> My brand promise: accurate, in-depth research delivered with charm and persistence.
>
> My brand essence: accuracy, conscientiousness and respect for others.

And now Joe, health club manager:

> Words that describe me: fit, active, fun to have around, ambitious, entrepreneurial, persuasive, responsive to sales targets, experienced in leading teams, enjoy being a boss, willing to take risks, like the limelight, experienced, skilled, talented fitness instructor, active in equestrian sports in spare time, special interest in cardiac fitness and 'prescription' sport for people with serious health problems.
>
> My brand promise: fitness for all is my aim and I'll stop at nothing (legal) to make it happen.
>
> My brand essence: fitness with fun, sales with energy and flair.

What are your own brand promise and brand essence?

| Description |
| --- |
| Brand promise |
| Brand essence |

## Your brand and the internet

When an employer is interested in you as a candidate, something like 70 per cent of them will Google your name. This will bring up any information held about you on the internet, including your pages on social networking sites such as Facebook, Twitter and LinkedIn. There is more about this in Chapter 3, but essentially you have to manage your brand on these pages as carefully as you manage it on paper or on any formal CV you submit. If your Facebook page has hilarious photographs of you jumping naked into a fountain, or lurching about drunkenly at a Christmas party, this will most probably mean the end of you as a candidate. If you are a fan of Twitter, then your tweets should be embarrassment free. Where you have a blog under your own name and have been indiscreet about your current employer, this will not be a recommendation to any possible new employer. You can, of course, delete such indiscretions, but unfortunately there is readily available software which will reveal the deleted material to anyone persistent enough to investigate. The answer is to be extremely careful about anything at all that you put online as it will be there, in effect, for ever.

## Deploying your brand

The most important immediate use for your brand identity is to check that any job you are applying for is actually a positive match with it. Only go ahead if it is clear that the environment, the skills and motivation that the job needs are a good fit. Most immediately, the work you have done in thinking through your brand will help you write the personal profile, if you decide to have one, as the opening paragraph of your CV (Chapter 8). Remember that brand identity is about being authentic – it's not about pretending but it is about being the very best version of yourself. It needs to convey the value you believe you will add for the employer. It will be clear what problems you can solve for the employer – and how. You now have to make sure that everything in your CV reflects this brand: what you say about yourself, how it is written and how it looks. Assuming you get on the shortlist, how you dress for the interview and other assessment process must also be consistent with what you have taken so much trouble to convey on paper.

# RESEARCHING THE EMPLOYER AND THE JOB

If you truly want to give yourself an advantage over other candidates, then you must do what few of them will do: research the potential employer and also take some time decoding what employers say about what they want. This chapter is about how to do the research that will make a difference.

## The case for research

Research forces you to focus on one or two prospective employers rather than assuming that it is all right to send the same old CV to all of them. It gives you an overview of their business and is a reminder that the only purpose of a job is to solve some problem that would otherwise be causing the business more serious problems. What you discover during the research process should filter into how you make your sales pitch (which is essentially what a CV is) and especially into how you write your covering letter or how you might offer any other add-ons (Chapters 10 and 11) to support your application. It plays to employer vanity because it shows that you have taken an interest in them, something all employers believe they are entitled to. At the very least, it is a fine way of checking out whether you really want to go ahead with the application. Even the simplest research will tell you something about the downsides of working in any organization, and while you should certainly take what you discover with a degree of scepticism, it will alert you to anything that needs investigation later. When you are an impressive applicant, thanks in part to this research, you will need to do much deeper and more extensive research to prepare for the interview, but you will already have a head start and a much clearer idea of where to look for more depth while other candidates are still at the beginning.

## The case against research

It can feel as if you are wasting your time until you know you have been shortlisted, and this lack of motivation can filter into the process or mean that you cause yourself endless delays about whether to apply or not. Of course, you have to be realistic. It is certainly true that you could be wasting your time if you are not shortlisted. However, if you fail to do any research, you reduce your chances of being shortlisted anyway. It's a gamble that you must decide to take or ignore.

## How and what to research

Start with what is openly available. This will include:

- The company's website.

- National press: search the business pages for mentions.

- Specialist press: look for articles in whatever the specialist journals are in the organization's field.

- Most organizations have their enemies, often disgruntled staff or customers. Try Googling 'the truth about < name of organization >' and see what comes up.

- Where the organization produces well-known services and products, Google 'customer reviews < name of organization >'.

- Regulators' reports: all public sector organizations are subjected to audit. Once you find out who the regulator is you can normally find the report on the regulator's website even if it is not on the organization's own site.

With this type of research you are looking for overarching themes. What does the organization say about themselves? How open do they seem? Do they make it easy to contact them? For instance, some websites have no information about who actually runs the company or their history. This is not necessarily sinister, but it does suggest that they have a degree of caution or unawareness. A website that is printed in minute type may hint that the organization does not actually want people to read what they say about themself. How well do they seem to be performing? All UK limited companies are registered with Companies House and you can search them through this route. Public limited companies (plcs) must give reports, including forecasts, to shareholders and are often the focus of articles in the business pages of newspapers. What are the trends in the financial results of the organization in which you are interested? How stable and profitable do they seem?

The more prominent an organization is, the easier it is to investigate their services. If your target organization is a major retailer, for instance, try going into one of the stores and imagine you are going in for the first time. What do you notice? Are the staff friendly? Do you have to wait an irritatingly long time for service or is it seamless and smooth? If you buy something and return it, how easy is this made for the customer? Where a building is publicly accessible, go in and ask for directions from Reception. Are they friendly and helpful? If you can wander around, as you can, for instance, in an NHS hospital, what general impression does the building give you? How do the staff look – are they scurrying around frowning or do they seem smiling and relaxed?

# Inside knowledge

Use your own network to track down people who currently work inside the organization or who have recently left. What is it actually like working there? How do people describe the 'culture' of the organization – that is, their hidden codes of conduct, what people are actually rewarded for as opposed to what the organization alleges is rewarded? Most organizations now conduct annual staff satisfaction surveys and these are extremely revealing. Ask an insider to send it to you: what does it tell you about the style of leadership or about how motivated and committed people are to the organization's stated aims? If there was a predecessor in the job, why have they left it?

## Talking to the contact named in the advertisement

Where there is a named person, often the HR person if it is an internal contact, or the recruitment consultant if it is being handled by an agency, then you should always take advantage of the offer to discuss the job. This discussion may be pitched in two ways: as a very informal first interview for the job (uncommon and also unfair unless it is described as essential in order to progress to the application stage, as not all candidates may take up the offer) or as an opportunity for you to find out a little more about what they want.

If it is an informal, brief screening, then it would be usual only to enquire into your qualifications and experience. Answer straight-forwardly. Don't seem overeager, just interested and alert.

Much more usually, this conversation is an opportunity to ask questions. Some good ones are:

What is the reason for the vacancy?

Who would the successful candidate report to?

How would you judge the performance of the successful candidate after six months?

What would have changed for the better as a result of having this person in post?

Ideally, what experience will the successful candidate have had in their career so far?

What are the absolutely essential skills that the successful candidate must have?

Don't make the mistake of assuming that this is a selling conversation; see it as fact finding that will help you decide whether or not to proceed with your application and how to shape the application if you do decide to go ahead. You should note that failing to contact the named person may count against you if and when you do decide to go ahead and apply, as it may be deemed to be lack of interest and initiative.

# Decoding the advertisement

A job application is always going to be much more persuasive and powerful if it is clear to the person receiving it that you have understood what they want. One of the ways of doing this is to spend time decoding the advertisement. Ads that look similar often turn out not to be when you spend a little time on this task. In fact, the employer may be looking for a significantly different person in each case.

To illustrate this point, I have taken two jobs loosely based on jobs advertised on the same agency website. Both call the job by the same title: Personal Assistant to a Head of Department, and both are based in central London, but looking carefully it is clear that different qualities and experience are needed for each.

*Job 1*

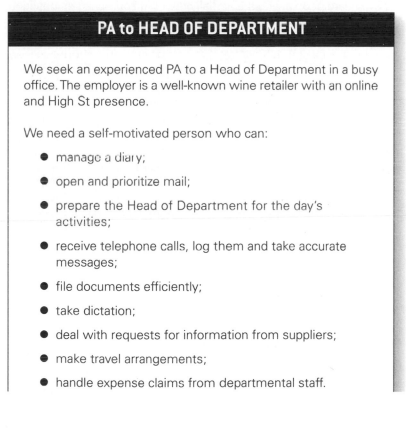

## PA to HEAD OF DEPARTMENT

We seek an experienced PA to a Head of Department in a busy office. The employer is a well-known wine retailer with an online and High St presence.

We need a self-motivated person who can:

- manage a diary;
- open and prioritize mail;
- prepare the Head of Department for the day's activities;
- receive telephone calls, log them and take accurate messages;
- file documents efficiently;
- take dictation;
- deal with requests for information from suppliers;
- make travel arrangements;
- handle expense claims from departmental staff.

**Desirable:** good spoken and written French or Spanish; experience of updating intranet or internet pages; previous experience of the wine trade.

**Essential:** at least 3 years' experience as PA to a senior manager, good knowledge of Word 2010, Excel, numeracy, dictation at level of 60 wpm.

What is really being sought here? The advertisement suggests that the employer is actually looking for someone more like a traditional secretary than a personal assistant, despite the use of the meaningless phrase 'self-motivated'; but the word secretary is rarely used these days – the job title itself has been promoted. The reference to a 'senior manager' is vague – never let something like this put you off. I have heard people who are actually rather junior managers describe themselves proudly as 'senior', so the word does not have any exact meaning. One possible giveaway is that this seems to be a boss who is not themself computer literate, relying on dictating (shorthand now being a bit of a vanishing art), and this boss also seems to need nanny-like care in preparing for the day ahead. Much of what the ad lists seems reactive: opening post and prioritizing it sounds like just making a nice neat pile for the boss. Note that the more responsible job of managing the boss's inbox is not mentioned. The phone calls are merely being 'logged' and the messages passed on – the PA does not sound as if they are expected to take any action as a result. The filing has to be done 'efficiently'. The travel arrangements, however, sound as if something a little livelier is expected.

The person who knows something about wine and can also speak one of the two languages is obviously going to have an advantage, along with someone who is confident that they either can already, or can learn how to, update internet or intranet pages.

Would this be your job?

Since this is a job advertised by an agency, there may be a limit to the research you can do, but if a named person is handling the appointment you can call them and check out the impressions the ad has given you. If indeed this is a job where the salary is reasonable because ideally they want someone with linguistic skills but it is also a job with a low level of daily responsibility and a great deal of routine, you might want to consider whether this is the right job for you.

If it is, in applying, your CV should stress your:

- high levels of organizing skills and comfort with filing, message taking;
- accuracy and detail focus as this will be essential for taking messages effectively;
- experience of making travel arrangements;
- numeracy: good arithmetical skills will be needed to check those expenses as well as understanding what the allowance system allows;
- shorthand speed and experience, especially if it is recent, as many people may have had training in shorthand but their actual skills are a little rusty;
- ability to support a boss in getting a detailed grasp of what they will be doing in any given day;
- ability to manage a boss relationship skilfully;
- IT skills with Word 2010 and Excel.

All the above are skills and experience that the majority of candidates will also have – or claim to have. You can hugely increase your chances of being shortlisted by emphasizing:

- Your knowledge of the language(s) named and spelling out what level of attainment you have. So instead of just 'knowledge of Spanish', say exactly what knowledge and skill you have: for instance, 'fluent in conversational Spanish with good accent and command of current idiom'. If you have been formally rated or examined, then you should add this: for instance, 'Professional Working Efficiency, Level 3 on the ILR rating system' and hope the employer knows what this means.
- Your interest in and knowledge of the wine trade, even if this is or was in a more junior or secondary capacity than the level needed for this job.

## Job 2

At a quick glance this job looks similar:

### Personal Assistant to Head of Department

The organization needs a skilled and experienced PA reporting to a Head of Practice in a high-profile law firm. This is a business unit which has to meet demanding targets and in this job you will be a key player. The core purpose of the role is to support the Head of < xxxxx > Practice.

Essential capabilities:

- able to manage relationships with other Heads and stakeholders;
- resilience;
- very highly organized and efficient, can maintain a smooth-running office under pressure;
- able to deal skilfully with senior colleagues of all sorts, especially senior lawyers inside and outside the Practice.

The job:

- Act as gatekeeper to the Head's diary; arrange meetings.
- Manage his inbox.
- Take minutes at meetings.
- Draft letters.
- Book travel in UK and abroad.
- Event management including large conferences and meetings.
- Process timesheets for the Practice team.
- Analyse data using Excel.
- Produce PowerPoint presentations to a high standard.

Experience in a legal practice desirable but not essential.

The overlap with the first job seems to be the areas of looking after the boss, diary management and processing team time sheets/ expenses, but it is clear when you look at it carefully that this is a more demanding job. It is genuinely a PA job. The person doing it will have to have an intimate understanding of their boss's life and preoccupations in order to make sensitive decisions about who gets access to them and who is politely put off, so will need high levels of diplomacy and confidence. Inbox management means being in on all the boss's secrets and being unafraid to answer on their behalf and also to know when this will not be appropriate. Minute taking is a high-level art because it means identifying the most important points in a meeting and then being able to write them all up clearly, tactfully and accurately. Event management is demanding and needs steady, focused organizing ability: managing the complicated logistics including who is invited and how, catering, speakers, visual displays, suppliers, venues, costs. It is probably no less than the truth that such a job will be pressured and will need someone with a cool head in order to do it successfully.

One giveaway when comparing job 1 with job 2 is that job 2 pays around 35 per cent more and offers a salary at the highest end of the PA spectrum.

So in applying for job 2, your CV would need to look very different from the CV needed for job 1. It would need to stress your skills and achievements, with examples, in:

- managing a relationship with a boss who has trusted you with complete diary and inbox management;

- maintaining confidentiality;

- minute taking;

- juggling many people's diaries to arrange meetings: evidence of persistence and tact plus high levels of comfort with detail;

- event management;

- producing PowerPoint slides – this most probably means working with words written by someone else, fitting them to an existing organizational template, and probably researching and adding graphics as well;

- keeping cool under the pressure of so many demands;

- your confidence, tact and natural authority in dealing with professionals such as solicitors and barristers, many of whom are known for their reluctance to be 'managed'.

Although previous experience in a legal environment is not listed as a 'must', it is obvious that to have it would be a distinct advantage. My guess would also be that job 2 is a much more formal environment and therefore demands an ultra-smart appearance and formal business clothing, whereas this may not matter quite so much with job 1.

One mistake made by many job applicants is to assume that the employer will know what an applicant means by, for instance, their claims to be 'an experienced PA'. One of my clients said to me in puzzlement that she could not understand why she had been rejected for such a job on the basis of her 'lack of experience'. 'But I told them I had loads!' she said; and indeed she did. When I looked at the CV she had submitted, what she had done was to describe herself as experienced, leaving it at that, assuming that the employers could work out for themselves that this meant she could organize an office, order stationery, do filing, navigate the internet and deal with diaries. Unfortunately employers do not make these assumptions. If they list the duties and qualities they want, then you have to spell out for them exactly how you match their requirements.

If experience or knowledge is listed that you do not have, then it is always worth stressing your ability to learn quickly and your willingness to devote time and energy to the task of doing it. So, for instance, if you consider yourself to be internet and IT savvy but have yet to learn how to update an internet page, you could write something like:

I am a confident internet user with high levels of IT awareness and skill and am certain that I could very rapidly learn how to update your website pages.

## Shortlisting: how employers use CVs

In theory the days are gone when employers merely trusted to gut instinct when looking at a CV. This is not because their attitudes have really changed, only that their terror of being taken to a tribunal has produced changes in behaviour. Decisions now have to be justified, including whether to shortlist a candidate or not. This is why when the HR professional takes a so-called 'long-list' to the hiring manager, they will have prepared a document to make the task as quick and easy as possible. So if we take the first of the two sample jobs, the shortlisting table might look like this:

| Name of candidate | |
| --- | --- |
| Experience: essential | |
| Been a PA to senior manager for 3 years minimum | |
| Diary management | |
| Handling post | |
| Filing | |
| Dictation at least 60 wpm | |
| Word 2010 | |
| Excel | |
| Travel management | |
| Desirable | |
| Intranet / internet page updates | |
| French / Spanish | |
| Knowledge of wine trade | |

Unless you can tick all the 'essential' boxes and at least one of the 'desirable' ones, it is probably not worth your while to apply as it is unlikely that you will be shortlisted.

## Job descriptions and person specifications

When you apply for a job through an agency, you may be given only minimal information about the role because the agency will be keen to stop candidates approaching the employer directly, thus cutting out their fee. It is always worth asking if there is a job description as this will give you further information, helping you strengthen your application as well as decide whether you want to go ahead with it.

Jobs that are advertised directly by the employer will usually offer a job information pack which will contain background information about the organization and recruiting department as well as a job description and 'person specification'.

The job description is a document listing the purpose of the job and accountabilities of the post holder; good practice is to describe no more than eight accountabilities for a junior job and no more than 12 for a senior one. 'Accountabilities' is a jargon word which means 'this is what you would be responsible for' – ie how you will be held to account. It describes how the purpose of the job is to be achieved. The art of writing crisp, clear job descriptions seems to be one which many employers lack. I have seen job descriptions which go on for several pages and which are simply tedious lists of tasks, making it impossible to distinguish the trivial and obvious from the true priorities. Sometimes the job description will also contain useful clues, buried deep inside it, to what the employer is looking for in terms of skills and qualities. Job descriptions do matter because they are the foundation of the company's contract with their employee, making it clear what is expected, allowing pay to be awarded fairly and openly and as a basis for personal development. Usually the job description will say where the role sits in the structure, where it is physically based and to whom the person reports. It will then list the responsibilities, typically describing:

- any staff who have to be managed;
- organizing and planning duties; tasks needing to be done;
- information that has to be communicated and to whom;
- monitoring and reporting: what, how and to whom;
- quality control.

## Example

An agricultural machinery manufacturer is looking for a sales and marketing person. They have advertised the job as a suitable place for a young graduate with an engineering degree to start a career in sales. This is how the job description looks:

Job title: Agricultural Machinery Sales and Marketing Executive

Reports to: Marketing Director

Based: Leicester

Job purpose: Telephone sales to dealer network; providing general customer support and technical back-up

Key responsibilities:

- Answer customer queries re whole range of products.
- Deal with and resolve customer complaints.
- Carry out agreed number of direct sales calls daily to dealer network.
- Follow up sales calls, liaising with field sales team.
- Access and update customer relations management (CRM) software.
- Research competitors' products and offers.
- Keep product knowledge up to date at all times.
- Attend training as required.

The company has also produced a person specification. This spells out what kind of experience and skill the ideal candidate will have. A person specification usually covers these areas: qualifications, experience, skills, physical requirements (for instance, in terms of health and strength), and any travel that is necessary – and this again will be used as part of the recruitment process. Initially it will be used to decide whether to shortlist you or not. When you are shortlisted, it will guide the questions you are asked at the interview, or, as is increasingly common, at an assessment centre where you might encounter a range of activities designed to test whether you have the skills you claim and that the employer needs. The form the employer uses at this stage and for the job in agricultural sales might look like this and might also be sent to you so that the process is totally transparent:

| Person Specification for Agricultural Machinery Sales and Marketing Executive | | | |
|---|---|---|---|
| Name of candidate | How assessed | | |
| Qualities and experience | CV | A/centre | Interview |
| Communication: persuasive telephone manner; ability to create rapport immediately | | • | • |
| Written communication: high standard of literacy; able to write brief, accurate reports | • | • | • |
| Social confidence: can create impression of friendly authority | | • | • |
| Sales experience, not necessarily in a direct sales environment | • | | |
| Enthusiastic, ambitious, self-motivated, responds to targets | • | • | • |
| Team player | • | • | |
| Familiarity with the agricultural environment | • | | • |
| Degree in mechanical engineering or similar | • | | |
| IT: can use Word and Excel | • | | |
| Willing to relocate to Leicester | • | | |
| Self-motivated learner; can acquire new knowledge quickly | • | | • |

In applying for this job, you would need to make sure that your CV pays scrupulous attention to each of the items on the person specification, double-checking with the job description, where further information often lurks about what the employer is really looking for. Where the employer specifically lists a high standard of written communication as part of the person specification, as in the job above, it is especially important to ensure that the CV is well written and typo-free (Chapter 12). It is no good claiming that you write well if your CV gives immediate evidence that you do not.

## Competencies

You may also encounter the word 'competencies' on a person specification as well as in requests on application forms to give examples of how you have particular competencies.

Competency is an HR word used to describe a bundle of attributes, skills and experience which can be demonstrated reliably and at a consistently high standard. The competency might have the same label – for instance, team working – but the definition might vary according to whether the job was at a junior or senior level. In practice, most competency lists are remarkably similar. In any managerial or professional job, including those at entry level, you can expect to see these:

leadership;

analytical thinking;

financial acumen;

communication: written and oral;

influencing/persuasiveness;

decision making;

planning and organizing;

problem solving;

IT skills;

self-management;

teamwork;

managing performance.

Usually the employer will give you a brief definition of what they mean by the competency. So persuasiveness might be defined in the person specification as:

being assertive; remaining calm and tactful even when under pressure; able to make a convincing argument; able to listen without getting defensive; can reach an agreement which meets everyone's needs; willingness to compromise while also able to protect your own interests.

Competencies are used in selection on the principle that your past behaviour is a reliable guide to how you might perform in future, so the employer is more interested in *how* you did something than in *what* you did or in what you promise you could do in the future.

So when you see competencies listed in a person specification it is important to give examples of situations where you were calling on that competency and to phrase your examples in a way that follows the employer's format.

When you assemble all the information you have about a job, print it off and use a highlighter on the key words, whether they are in the original advertisement, the background briefing on the organization, the job description or the person specification. Don't start assembling your CV until you have done this and listed all the words that emerge. They will form the foundation of the specially crafted CV that you will now produce as your application for the job. Doing this and using the employer's own vocabulary will show the care you have taken to match what you offer to what the employer needs. This hugely increases the chances that your CV will be put on the read-more-carefully pile and of your being put on the shortlist for interview.

# 6

# WHAT TO LEAVE OUT

There are fashions in CVs as in every other part of life and what was acceptable and necessary in the recent past is not always acceptable now. When you are struggling to reduce the length of a CV, it is useful to know what you can safely omit. There are exceptions to these 'rules' but this chapter contains general guidance on what you should leave out – and why.

## The heading 'Curriculum vitae'

There is no need to put 'Curriculum vitae' or 'CV' at the top of the first page because it will be obvious what the document is. But make sure the header or footer says < your name CV > along with the page number.

## Your date of birth

Don't give your date of birth. Using age as one of the selection criteria for a job has been illegal in the UK since 2006. In addition, from April 2011 the previous default statutory retirement age of 65 has been phased out. Asking for your date of birth used to be routine on application forms, though most employers are now wise to omit this in light of the legislation. Unlike US legislation, which is aimed at protecting older workers, the UK law protects workers of all ages – so, for instance, if the employer unreasonably excludes you because you are too young, you are protected as much as you would be if you were considered too old. The older you are, the more you may feel it is desirable to avoid giving the potential employer an instant excuse to exclude you; and equally, if you are apparently very young for a particular role, you can omit your date of birth for the same reason. Actually, of course, it is usually easy for the employer to work out your age from the dates of your qualifications, assuming you got them at the usual life stages.

## Your driving licence

The status of your driving licence only matters if driving is an essential part of the job. Disclosing speeding convictions or telling the employer how many points you have or have had on your licence is also irrelevant unless it is specifically asked for and justifiable legally. I once saw a draft CV for an administrative and entirely office-based job that not only disclosed far more information about the candidate's driving history than any employer could possibly wish to know, but also gave his driving licence number.

## Getting too personal

Never offer information on your credit status, citizenship, passport number or national insurance number. Where you were born is irrelevant. The employer does not need to know your mother's maiden name or your parents' occupations. Your ethnic origin may be asked for as part of a monitoring process, but never offer it on your CV. Marital status is neither here nor there. The employer does not need to know if you are single, divorced, remarried, currently between boyfriends or girlfriends, engaged, homosexual with or without a civil partner, and with no children or a large tribe. Other irrelevancies: the names of your children, the quirky names of your pets, the fact that you keep rabbits, horses or love cats, your partner's occupation and how long you have been together. The employer is not interested in your weight, height or skin colour. Your religious beliefs are an entirely private matter.

The other reason for omitting your date of birth, details about your driving licence, passport and parentage applies especially to posting a CV on the internet. You may eventually be asked for some of these details when you are offered the job, for instance to reassure the employer that you are legally entitled to work in the UK. But these details can be an invitation to fraud when they are openly available: as an example, it could be possible to obtain a credit card on the basis of a driving licence and full name alone. If you are asked for such details on a website, take this as a sign of highly dubious activity.

## Photographs: leave them out

Photographs may be essential on an internet dating site or as part of your page on a social networking site, but they have no place in a CV. One client showed me a draft CV which had a photograph of herself dressed in an impressive hat and frock, showing off the OBE she had just received at Buckingham Palace. While this was a moment of justifiable pride in her life, it looked out of place on a CV. When I asked her to get opinions from a few friends to check out my own feedback she reported back with great hurt that one person had said 'It goes to show that OBE stands for Other Buggers' Efforts.' Her photograph risked provoking just such jealous and irrational responses in an employer. Similarly you might not get the reaction you expect if your photograph shows you as a man with a moustache and long hair or a woman with a tad too much make-up for the personal taste of the recruiter.

Asking for photographs is extremely unusual in the UK not least because powerful anti-discrimination laws mean that an employer could be accused of bias – for instance, a candidate might claim that they had been rejected because the photograph showed they were brown skinned. Photographs are essential in casting directories, where how you look does matter, but they have no place in a CV unless you are a performer of some sort, where a carefully chosen photograph is permissible.

## Training courses: mostly they are irrelevant

Many people extend their CVs unnecessarily by listing all the training courses they have attended. I saw one CV where the candidate seemed admirably committed to her own development and took up the best part of a page to list every course she had undertaken over a three-year period, ranging from a half-day health and safety seminar to a four-day event on managing conflict, with brief descriptions of each. This had the opposite effect from the one she intended. It suggested that she was more interested in being a course attendee than in doing her job or that she was hopelessly unready for her job and had needed the courses to remedy unfortunate deficits in her skills.

The main reason for not bothering with listing courses is that going on a course does not guarantee that anything in your behaviour will have changed. Where a course has involved some kind of assessment, and you have passed it, then it appears in your list of qualifications anyway.

## *Exceptions*

Some courses are high profile and are worth mentioning if more than one of these features applies:

- You had to compete to get a place.
- The course is known for the demands it makes on participants.
- It cost big money (£10,000+).
- The institution itself has cachet – for instance, it is a respected business school such as INSEAD, Harvard, the London Business School or a think tank such as The King's Fund.
- The course was longer than five days and therefore involved significant commitment on your own part to attend.
- The course has a serious social as well as developmental aim – for instance the Common Purpose courses.
- It had a major impact on your own professional development.
- You funded it yourself or won a bursary.

## Schools and early education: no one cares

It's no wonder that some CVs are so long when they start with every single detail of education, including primary school. Some people name their schools because they think that a famous school will graciously bestow its status, but again, this may have unintended negative effects. As we see with high-profile politicians, attending Eton may actually give the child a head start in life, but it also suggests that your parents have bought privilege – and for people not so lucky, this may mean that it provokes hostility. In fact, I usually advise clients to omit school details altogether as it is qualifications that matter rather than where you went to school. When you list qualifications you also list the name of the institution, so the employer can see which university or higher education establishment you attended. If you are a graduate and over 30, with several years of employment as part of your experience, then the employer will take it for granted that you have A levels and GCSEs, so it uses up space pointlessly to include such details. If you did not enter higher education, or are a young graduate seeking a first proper job, then it can be helpful to give dates and names of your GCSEs and A levels.

## Your current or last salary: don't disclose it

When you are job searching, salary will be one of the features which decide whether you apply or not. Roughly speaking, employers expect you to be earning within plus or minus 10 per cent of the salary they are offering. It may put them off if this is not the case. One jobseeker who had been earning a generous six-figure sum for many years found that disclosing his former salary was a deterrent to potential employers. They either thought that he was unlikely to stay when his previous remuneration had been so high, or felt he might be overqualified for the role. At 66 and having been made redundant in a declining sector, there was now little demand for some of his skills and knowledge. He had to scale down his ambitions in order to get work and was happy to do so. He revealed his former salary only when actually offered the new job. If your current salary is significantly less than the one the employer is offering, it may spoil your chances of being taken seriously if it appears on your CV: Why is this junior person applying for this job with us?

Similarly, omit any details of grade and hierarchy. These will mean nothing to people outside your current organization and will convey that you have become thoroughly institutionalized, the kind of person who is unlikely to be able to make a smooth transition to a new job and organization.

# Too much detail about much earlier jobs

Employers have a sliding scale of interest in your career history. They are extremely interested in your current or last job, slightly interested in the job before that and have only the most cursory interest in what you did more than two jobs or seven years ago, whichever is the greater period of time. Your earlier career history will certainly show them what the thread in your career has been but if you are now in your forties and working as a public sector middle manager, it is unlikely that any new employer will wish to know that as a 20-year-old you worked as an office assistant in the local brewery. Unless the job is unusual, it is often obvious what the duties were anyway: for instance, if you were a secretary, a retail sales assistant, a police constable, a teacher in a primary school or a front-line social worker, most people will feel they know what you did. Your CV should reflect this, with most attention paid to the current job and about two-thirds less space on the previous job, tailing off to bare essentials for jobs before that.

# Accounting for earlier career

Use any of these tactics, depending on how long your career has been and the nature of the path it reveals:

- List the name of the employer, the job and the dates, devoting about 40 words to your responsibilities and main achievements – no more than three jobs to be given this treatment.

- Just give the list without any descriptions.

- Write: 'Previous jobs included:'. Then list them, without dates or names of employers.

- Write: 'Earlier career: details on request.' And be prepared to give them if the prospective employer asks.

# Why you left your last job: keep this to yourself

There is no need to state your reasons for leaving a job. This is particularly true if there was some conflict with the employer (see also Chapter 13). There are any number of reasons for leaving a job:

boredom, lack of opportunities for promotion, needing to earn more money, you fell out with your boss, your partner got promoted and you had to follow him or her to another part of the country, you were made redundant, you had to leave on health grounds, you were sacked. All but a few of these motives are unflattering to the candidate. If you give a reason for leaving one job, then you have to give it for all of them, and this could put you at a disadvantage. The exception is where you have been unlucky enough to be employed successively by companies that went bust or downsized dramatically. Here your CV could then show many changes of job in an unusually short time and you may wish to add a brief explanation in brackets such as 'company restructured' or 'company went into administration'.

## Referees: offer them only if asked

It used to be the case that CV writers automatically included the names of two referees. These typically were the names of people intended to impress the reader with the fame or status of the referee. Sometimes, the famous person has not been asked for their consent and so may refuse when approached. When the famous person does not know the CV writer at all well, but may think of them kindly, they will still only be able to give the vaguest, briefest and most general of comments so will not necessarily help your cause. Also, the referee may not be as respected as the CV writer believes – so, for example, a candidate who includes the name of a celebrated and controversial politician as one of their referees risks provoking the wrath of a reader who does not share their own reverence for this individual.

However, the main reason for not including referees is that normally the employer will now only approach referees if they are about to offer you the job. This is because seeking references for everyone on the shortlist takes up time that the employer can ill afford. Written references have also become devalued, with reference writers wary of being sued, for instance for malicious defamation, if they are less than wholly enthusiastic about the candidate, refusing to give more than the barest details of where and how the person was employed and at what salary. Prospective employers are much more likely to ask at the job offer stage for tightly specified people who can be interviewed by phone – for instance, your current or last line manager – and to check that the referee is who they say they are rather than a best mate in some fictitious role who has been primed to speak highly of the candidate in return for a few beers.

Always ask the referee's permission before giving their name, and do so for each and every job. I have sometimes been asked to give references on a blank-cheque basis, in other words for any future job for which the candidate may apply and have always refused, even where I am happy to endorse an application for a specific job. A referee may feel they do not know enough about a prospective job to give a view or may consider that they do not know you well enough to be able to say or write anything sensible about how ably you would fit that particular role. It will repay the small investment of time on your part to call any referee and brief them on the job, help them understand what it involves and what it will be useful for them to say. Sometimes the referee may ask you to draft the reference. If so, that's fine – it's up to them whether they use your words or not. In the interests of openness, and because I dislike unnecessary secrecy, I always send candidates a copy of what I have said about them and I believe this to be good practice, but I gather it is unusual. The employer will, of course, send referees the job information, but most referees will be too busy to read much of it, so your own guidance will be essential.

Never attach testimonials – those 'To whom it may concern' statements which praise you lavishly. Employers are likely to discard or disregard such documents as spin, not least because, if genuine, they often go back many years into the past and therefore have little relevance to the here and now, or the employer knows that they have so often proved fraudulent, composed by the candidate themself.

## Exceptions

For some jobs you will have to declare personal details that are not required in the normal run of CV writing. For such careers, for instance in medicine or nursing, you will usually have to fill in an application form which will clarify what information you need to give. Any profession for which you need a licence to practise will probably ask you to submit to this degree of scrutiny, asking you for the PIN of your registration details and dates by month and year of every single employer because career gaps could indicate something sinister. They will ask for evidence of continuing professional development (CPD) and for proof that your licence is still current or that you have current Criminal Records Bureau (CRB) clearance. Other careers, for instance in government, may need security clearance, but this will be made clear at the stage when you are just enquiring, so it is up to you whether you take your application forward or not, knowing that you will be asked for a level of personal disclosure which could be uncomfortable.

# 7

# WORD MAGIC

CV language is not like normal ways of writing and speaking. In fact, it is a little world of its own and you need to learn how to manage your way through it. Your task in writing the CV is to pack as much power as possible into two pages. A CV is a formal document. It is not the place for the chatty style of a blog, the carefree typos that a friend will forgive in a text or the sloppy punctuation that may sprinkle an e-mail. This chapter introduces you to the special code of CV language and describes how to make maximum impact in the fewest possible words.

## Banning 'I' and 'me'; eliminating definite articles

One common mistake is to use 'I', 'me' and 'myself' throughout. The reader knows it is you because your name is at the top and bottom of the document. It begins to sound coy and boastful: I, me, myself – and more of me. Also it takes up space that you can ill afford. So your first task is to eliminate as many of the 'I's and 'me's as you can. Some people suggest writing about yourself in the third person – that is, as if you are writing about someone else. This is a good idea for the informal, biography-style CV (page 128) but strikes the wrong note in a formal CV. Instead, just banish the first person.

You should also get rid of definite and indefinite articles – 'the', 'a' and 'an' – and wherever possible, words like 'and'. Yes, it may give a staccato impression but remember your aim is to communicate the maximum information in the shortest possible space.

Here is an example. First draft:

> I am confident as a communicator, and I have learnt how to deliver information in a range of formats and styles to suit the audience. I have taught myself how to make management presentations and do verbal briefings. Also I have an eye for detail and have experience of both editing and proofreading copy. (54 words)

Rewritten without the I-word and definite and indefinite articles, this is how it looks:

> Confident communicator able to deliver information in range of formats and styles to suit audience, whether management presentations or verbal briefings. Strong eye for detail with experience of editing and proofreading. (31 words)

Here is another example. First attempt:

> I ran the Syndication Department at News Chronicle's Headquarters Building for three years, increasing our sales internationally by 55% and securing four major new clients in Australia and New Zealand and obtaining senior management backing to increase the sales force from 4 to 8. (44 words)

Second attempt:

> Ran News Chronicle's Syndication Department for three years, gaining senior management backing for doubling sales force, increasing international sales by 55%, securing four major new Australasian clients. (27 words)

# Eliminate feeble words

Banish the faintly apologetic and modest language of normal British speech. Strip out all those modifying words which can imply tentativeness and uncertainty in a CV: *quite*, *rather*, *very*, *about*, *pretty* (as in *pretty good*), *nearly*, *almost*, *fairly*, *slightly*, *somewhat*, *really*.

For instance, a candidate who was an experienced nurse with a rock-solid track record wanted to write this on her CV: 'I am quite good at working on a high-dependency ward and have about a year of

ITU experience.' How did this seem to a casual reader? Unconfident, vague and insecure – which this person was not. She rewrote it as:

> Eight years of experience on high-dependency ward and ten months' experience of ITU.

Similarly, eliminate verbs such as *have*, *had*, *was*, *got*. They lack power. For instance, a young teacher looking for a promotion in a different school wrote as her first draft:

> I have had 2 years of Year 1 experience with an intake from a catchment area of severe social deprivation and this has given me broad and deep experience of how to deal with difficult classroom behaviour

Rewritten, this version had more crispness:

> Two years of Year 1 teaching with intake from area of severe social deprivation. Broad and deep experience of successfully handling challenging classroom behaviour.

Other useless words include *would*, *could*, *might*, as in:

> I would point out that I won the prize for customer care in the month of June last year.

> I might say that I have expertise in horticulture gained while at college, graduating in 2009.

These sentences would be better written as:

> Won the June 2011 customer care prize.

> Expert horticulturalist, qualified 2009.

# Get rid of the passive voice

In an effort to make a CV sound more impressive, many people use the passive voice. So they write sentences such as:

> The department was reorganized in order to make savings of 12% on costs.

The effect is pompous and results in flabby language. It is much less clear what the writer is trying to say – everything seems as if it is at one remove and the result is a noncommittal statement. Stick to the active voice by putting the verb at the beginning of the sentence:

Reorganized department, making cost savings of 12%.

## Demonstrating your experience

Inexperienced CV writers often take up the whole document describing their responsibilities. A typical example would be a middle-ranking health service nurse-manager whose CV followed this pattern:

June 2008–present: Unit Manager, Neonatal Department, University of X NHS Trust, < city name >.

The Unit has 21 intensive cots and 25 high-dependency cots and receives babies with severe problems: renal, cardiac, neurological, metabolic, respiratory. Job involves:

bed management and allocation;

liaising with A&E and Maternity Unit;

liaising with surgical teams;

providing high-dependency and intensive care for neonates;

developing and managing care pathways;

offering clinical leadership to other nurses.

The problem is that while this describes the impressive responsibilities, it does not answer the question that all employers ask, which is: 'OK, this is what your job description says you do, but so what? How are you doing it? What difference have you made?' A reader will have no idea whether you actually carried out these responsibilities let alone how well you carried them out. You could be the world's most successful Jobsworth.[1] Employers want someone who will do more than just fulfil the obligations laid down in the job description.

# Writing about how you made a difference: vocabulary

Look for words that suggest dynamism, creativity, leadership and change, especially in the part of the CV where you are setting out your skills and attainments. Employers are always looking for people who can demonstrate benefits. These are areas such as:

| Increase | Decrease | Improve |
| --- | --- | --- |
| profit/surplus | sickness absence | competitiveness |
| staff retention | losses and deficits | collaboration, eg with suppliers |
| staff morale | cycle time | relationships – inside and outside the organization |
| teamwork | waste | communication |
| efficiency | costs | innovation rate |
| creativity | delays | bottom-line results |

If you can demonstrate that you have done any of these things, make sure that your CV says so.
  Here are some helpful words:

| | | |
| --- | --- | --- |
| analysed | generated | oversaw |
| conducted | guided | pioneered |
| coordinated | improved | produced |
| delivered | influenced | reshaped |
| developed | integrated | resolved |
| devised | introduced | restructured |
| directed | launched | reviewed |
| eliminated | led | stabilized |
| established | managed | streamlined |
| executed | modernized | trained. |
| facilitated | negotiated | |
| formulated | organized | |

# Use the power of numbers

Many CV writers ignore one of the most effective tools at their disposal: using numbers to emphasize claims about their experience and skill. For instance, compare these two phrases:

> Experienced online journalist.

> Eight years of successful online journalism.

Or these:

> Made significant overhead savings.

> Reduced overheads by 25%.

The second option is more powerful in each case. Wherever you can, quantify: use numbers, actual money, percentages.
Examples:

> Managed division with 75 staff.

> Reduced deficit to zero in two years.

> Improved market share by 25%.

> Reduced registration time for users from 6 days to 10 minutes through use of new IT system.

> Reduced sickness and absence levels from 18% to 8% in eighteen months by implementing new policy.

> Improved exam results with 30% increase in students obtaining A* grades.

> Increased voluntary donations from £10,000 to £35,000 within a year.

> Implemented new system, saving 20% on operating costs.

> Improved productivity of X department by 30% on the same budget.

> Increased user satisfaction by 10% over last year's results.

> Managed the opening of the new Youth and Play Centre within 3 days of contractors finishing; met target of recruiting 100 young members within first week.

This is the simplest way to show how you went beyond what your job asked of you.

# More about numbers

It has become accepted practice in normal writing to abbreviate big numbers, so that £45,000 becomes £45k and £2,000,000 becomes £2m. Don't do this in a CV. It is better to use the whole number or, if you are dealing in millions, to write £2 million because it has more impact. Similarly, use actual numbers and the percentage symbol rather than writing numbers as words (except at the beginning of a sentence) or using the words 'per cent': '10%' looks better on a CV than 'ten per cent'.

# The storytelling approach

For more senior jobs there is an even more powerful version. In effect what you do is tell a story in miniature. This will follow the structure of every story in the world, whether fairy tale, film, novel or play:

1 Things seem to be going along as usual.

2 Then there is a crisis of some kind where the consequences of not dealing with it would be horrible.

3 The hero or heroine has to take action in order to save the day.

4 How it ends: happily or unhappily.

In writing about this for CV purposes, you adapt it in this way:

1 A brief account of the situation before you tackled it.

2 What the crisis was and why it would have been bad for the organization had it continued unchecked.

3 Exactly how you tackled it – this should be the greater part of what you write.

4 The positive way it ended, using numbers wherever possible.

## Example 1

George is a PA looking for a better-paid and more responsible job. He works for a somewhat ditzy and highly talented senior executive in an independent film company. His job description says that he manages her diary, sets up meetings, does the filing, books travel, organizes catering and deals with purchase orders and invoicing, among many other familiar PA tasks – including many not mentioned in the job description, such as reminders of when her children's birthdays fall due. If George merely sets this out in his CV, he will definitely not stand out as a candidate because there is no way this list can convey the frenzied way his boss works or how he supports her.

George asks himself what he has increased, decreased or improved and the answer is 'a lot': people no longer have to wait six weeks to have their expense claims signed; suppliers' invoices are processed within 10 days rather than 10 weeks; there are no more embarrassing diary clashes where his boss finds two people arriving at the same time for entirely separate meetings, or indignant phone calls from people asking why she is not at some scheduled event; files can be retrieved within seconds rather than apparently disappearing for good. In writing about this, George is aware of the danger of appearing to criticize either his boss, of whom he is fond, or his predecessor, whom he does not know.

George takes the story structure and creates powerful items for his CV. Here is one example based on the improvements he made to managing her diary:

| Diary management | The heading: reflecting a duty the potential new employer has also named |
|---|---|
| Inherited situation where boss was frequently double-booked, causing inconvenience to her and colleagues | Combines stages 1 and 2 of the story format |
| Researched, purchased and installed new diary software, arranged remote access for her; trained boss and colleagues in use; took over all appointment making | Stage 3: emphasizes the initiative he took and what he actually did |
| New system now runs smoothly with clashes eliminated to zero | Stage 4: shows it was successful and how |

This will form one bullet in his CV under the heading 'Achievements', reading like this:

> **Diary management**. Inherited situation where boss was frequently double-booked, causing inconvenience to her and colleagues. Researched, purchased and installed new diary software, arranged remote access for her; trained boss and colleagues in use; took over all appointment making. New system now runs smoothly with clashes eliminated to zero.

## Example 2

Lezley is a senior HR professional working for a manufacturer of packaging. When she arrived in the job four years ago, the reputation of HR was at an all-time low. People grumbled that recruitment took far too long because it seemed snarled up in endless bureaucracy, that HR stopped things rather than progressing them and made little contribution to the business. Lezley has transformed HR in this company. Now she is ready to move on and is aiming for a job as HR director in a bigger organization where the role of HR as a business partner is well understood. The emphasis in the possible new job is on process improvement and on managing change, so this is what Lezley emphasizes in her CV. Here are two of her bullet points:

> **Process improvement**. Took over a poorly functioning recruitment function, operating in such cumbersome ways that key posts typically remained vacant for 16 weeks, costing business minimally £200k per annum. Moved on poor performers; recruited and trained new team in consultancy skills and customer responsiveness; created new software for online advertising and responding. Reduced recruitment cycle time to 5 weeks.

> **Talent management**. Developed succession-planning scheme for retaining and developing talent essential for future of business. Introduced assessment centres at selection stage. Improved staff retention on new hires from 50% to 95% over 4-year period.

## Example 3

Andrew has had a career in civil engineering and is now looking for a board-level job. In describing his current role in a niche company, he makes it clear that as director of operations, he rescued it from what looked like an inevitable bankruptcy:

Inherited situation where cost overruns on investment project put company at risk of bankruptcy. Drove down costs by 35%, sold non-essential assets, delivering value recovery of £400m, and restructured finances enabling creditors to recover their money and company to reinvest.

Hint: always start with the general and work from there to the particular. For instance, in the following example, it is all a bit of a jumble, making it difficult for a reader to see quickly what the task or skill actually was:

Listened to recordings of staff phone calls with customers and offered them feedback on how to improve, trained them in how to use basic scripts effectively, devised and ran training for newcomers, typically 5 staff over a 6-week period.

Rewriting it makes it clearer what the reader is supposed to take in first:

Trained 35 new staff a year in call handling, teaching them how to handle basic scripts, listening in to calls and offering feedback to improve their effectiveness.

Here the emphasis is on the main activity – training – rather than starting with how the training was done, as in the first example. You could make it even clearer by giving it a bulleted label:

● Training. Trained 35 new staff a year in call handling, teaching them how to handle basic scripts, listening in to calls and offering feedback to improve their effectiveness.

## Keep sentences short

Remember that your aim is for the reader to take in your messages as quickly as possible. Long, complex sentences make this more difficult. A manager who was also a finance specialist wanted to convey his commitment to coaching and mentoring with his team, but his first effort was hard to read because of the length and rambling construction of the sentence:

Mentoring internal non-finance professional staff to enable them to decode budgets and providing formal mentoring for non-finance managers was successful, so I have also adopted a coaching approach to management with strong encouragement of self-development and learning while setting clear targets, objectives and expectations.

His second attempt was much better because it was shorter, clearer and also split the original long sentence into two:

Mentored non-finance colleagues on understanding budgets. Adopted coaching approach to team, encouraging self-development against clear objectives.

## Keep the words short and simple

The English language draws on two main sources of words: French and Anglo-Saxon. French was the language of the 11th-century Norman invaders, and for several centuries French was the language of the aristocracy, the court, diplomacy, the justice system and government. The Normans brought around 10,000 such words with them. Before the invasion, English people spoke a form of Anglo-Saxon, a language of Germanic origin. Gradually the two languages became blended and modern English emerged in the 16th century. But the custom persists of using words of French origin when we want to seem official and serious. Many of these words typically end in -ion, -ate, -ise, -ize, -able, -ify. George Orwell wrote an essay on the English language in which he had some fun rewriting a well-known verse from Ecclesiastes. This is how the Good News Bible puts it:

I realized that in this world fast runners do not always win the race, and the brave do not always win the battle. Wise men do not always earn a living, intelligent men do not always get rich, and capable men do not always rise to high positions. Bad luck happens to everyone.

Orwell rewrote it in pompous jargon:

Objective considerations of contemporary phenomena compel the conclusion that success or failure in competitive activities exhibits no tendency to be commensurate with innate capacity, but that a considerable element of the unpredictable must invariably be taken into account.

As Orwell's tongue-in-cheek rewrite shows, the trouble with words of French origin is that they also tend to be long, with three or more syllables. In many cases there is a simpler, shorter word, often of Anglo-Saxon origin, that will do the job better. These are the words you should use in your CV wherever possible. Here are some examples:

| Word of French origin | Shorter alternative |
|---|---|
| approximately | about |
| accomplish | do |
| accurate | true |
| ameliorate | make better |
| appearance | look |
| acquire | buy |
| cessation | stopping |
| commence | start |
| compensation | payment |
| construct | build |
| correct | right |
| demonstrate | show |
| discuss | talk |
| enquire | ask |
| incorrect | wrong |
| inventory | stock |
| necessity | need |
| paradigm | pattern |
| permit | let |
| principal | main |
| procure | find/buy |
| purchase | buy |
| terminate | end |
| vocabulary | words |

In the last few years there has also been a trend to turn nouns that are already long into verbs, by adding -ise or -ize to them, or to turn already-long adjectives into nouns by adding -ity or -cy. So we get operationalize, optimize, incentivize, exceptionality, functionality, recency. Avoid such words; they are ugly.

Be sensible here. There are some words, for instance many in the list above (page 88) which are indeed of French origin and where there is no obvious substitute.

But the basic rule remains: choose short, simple words in preference to long complex ones wherever you can. There is compelling research evidence showing the positive impact that clear, simple language can have. The psychologist Daniel Oppenheimer asked people in a series of five studies to rate the intelligence of the writer based on the language they used in job applications and essays. He showed conclusively that the simpler the language, the more highly rated was the writer's supposed intelligence.[2]

## Jargon and buzz words

Jargon is different from legitimate technical terms. For instance, if you are a technician writing for other technicians in your field, technical terms are fine, though you should follow the useful rule of no more than one technical term for every 12 words. Technical terms are precise labels for technology, processes or ideas. Jargon means using language that is more complex than the words it replaces. So a 'supporting dentition device' is jargon for 'tooth splint'; 'diversity access installation' is jargon for putting in a ramp; 'multiple iterative consultations' is jargon for seeking opinions, and 'This train terminates at the next station stop' is jargon for 'All change at the next station.' We dislike jargon because we don't readily understand what it means and because the effect is to exclude. Jargon is used by professional groups and by corporate insiders to impress, to keep others at bay, or sometimes, more benignly, to communicate in shorthand. When you use it you imply that you, too, are on the inside. But beware:

- If you use insider's jargon before you are on the inside, you could annoy the reader – who may think you cheeky.

- You may not actually understand the true meaning of the jargon word.

- Where you have been thoroughly soused in an organization's culture for many years, you may forget that the words you use are jargon and you may not understand how they put off people who are not in on the secrets.

# Management jargon

Some jargon is just hideous and if a sentence has jargon piled upon jargon, the entire thing becomes clotted and incomprehensible. This applies particularly to management jargon. Here are a few examples – with translations:

| | |
|---|---|
| At the end of the day | Phrase which introduces a platitudinous thought such as 'Our staff are our biggest asset.' |
| Blue-sky thinking | Trying to get away from the usual ways of thinking about the organization's problems. Remarkably, no one ever talks about black-sky thinking. |
| Business model | Vague term which describes the underpinning assumptions of the business. |
| Buy-in | Saying yes. |
| Deliverables | Tasks. Organizations assign deliverables to their staff in the hope that this will motivate them. Alas, naming them deliverables does not make it any more likely that they will be delivered. |
| Eating your own dog food | Staff in the company start using their own services and discover why their customers are critical. |
| Low-hanging fruit | Not a pick-your-own sign but a phrase meaning tasks that are easily done. |
| Off-line | As in 'Let's talk about this offline,' meaning 'This is too embarrassing to talk about in public.' |
| Outputs | Management jargon often adds an 's' inappropriately in an attempt to give the idea more importance – eg trainings, learnings. In management jargon, 'outputs' means trying especially hard to achieve something, often an outcome. |
| Paradigm shift | Changing your mind by introducing a would-be smart new idea or model. |

| | |
|---|---|
| Robust | A word used by more junior managers who want to impress seniors with their toughness, as in 'We put robust measures in place,' meaning 'We threatened people with punishment if they did not deliver' (see deliverables, above). |
| To performance manage | Putting a member of staff through a disciplinary process that will end in their dismissal. |
| Rollout | Introducing yet another change programme into a change-weary organization. |
| Strategic envelope | Thinking long term, but exactly what contribution the envelope makes is not clear to me. |

When you write whole paragraphs of this stuff, you may think you are using the right buzz words, but it will still be difficult to understand, even by those who pen it themselves. Remember, too, that the chances are that your CV will be read first by the HR department and they are unlikely to be so familiar with the jargon and may simply conclude that you are a poor communicator. One of my clients wanted to include this horrible paragraph in his CV:

> I have managed multiple stakeholders within the strategic envelope, offering blue-sky thinking combined with rolling performance reviews to effect transformation.

It reads like a word game where you have to cobble together as many words as possible in one sentence. In fact, you could play with the words to make something equally unpleasant that would still leave any reader baffled:

> Blue-sky thinking in the strategic envelope where rolling performance reviews and combined stakeholders brought multiple transformation.

What this client meant was that he had high-level influencing skills, that he could manage groups with competing interests and that he had an impressive record in bringing about improvement for his organization – all of which was true. But there was no way he could have conveyed this successfully by writing it in the strangely contorted jargon of a management textbook. My advice is: banish jargon and write in English. I have never known anyone complain that a CV they received was too easy to read, but a great many employers have complained to me about the opposite.

## Great CV: shame about the typos

A whole generation seems to have grown up believing that spelling and punctuation no longer matter. Unfortunately, they do matter. If your CV contains a mass of typos, misspellings and hopeless punctuation, there will always be a reader who spots the mistakes. When people notice errors of this sort, they usually conclude any or all of the following: the perpetrator is uneducated, is sloppy, lacks conscientiousness. Skill in writing is essential for many jobs, certainly for all managerial jobs, so you will rule yourself out immediately if your CV contains mistakes of this sort. There are whole books devoted to grammatical accuracy and clear writing. The *Guardian* newspaper's *Style Guide*[3] is one of the most accessible and up to date but there are many others. There is no room in this book to cover all the possible traps. But here is a flavour of the sorts of things to look out for.

### *Homophones*

These are words which are pronounced identically but spelt differently and have different meanings. Spell checkers will not help here because to a computer the word will look fine. These are all examples I have seen on CVs:

accept (say yes): except (other than)

check (monitor progress): cheque (money)

complement (add to/make complete): compliment (praise)

council (assembly): counsel (advise)

discreet (hidden): discrete (separate)

principal (chief, senior): principle (a rule, a moral belief)

role (a part, a job): roll (a record, a list)

site (a place): cite (to quote or invoke an authority)

stationary (at a standstill): stationery (office supplies)

suite (a collection of something): sweet (confectionery, sweet taste).

Words which sound similar but have different meanings are another source of potential problems:

Affect means to influence. Effect when used as a verb means to put into practice.

Appraise means to evaluate. Apprise means to inform.

Alternate means by turns. Alternative means instead or a different option.

Prescribe means to recommend. Proscribe means to forbid.

Uninterested is not a substitute for disinterested. Disinterested means impartial.

## Common misspellings

These are the most commonly misspelt English words: *accommodate, definite, embarrassment, exceed, existence, gauge, harass, liaison, minuscule, millennium, necessary, parallel, personnel, precede, privilege, receive, separate, supersede*. Can you spell them all accurately? There are some words which change their spellings according to whether they are nouns or verbs. So you practise medicine (the verb form) but a doctor works out of a general practice (the noun). This is also an example of differences between British and US spelling. Americans use 'practice' for both forms. If you are competing for a job in a US company, change the spell check on your computer to US English.

Typos can easily creep in: fleid for field, nad for and, fo for of, and so on. Make full use of your spell checker: don't ignore those wavy red lines, and look out for words which are commonly mistyped and which the spell checker will not pick up – for instance, form for from or through for thorough.

You also need to be meticulous in checking how any company to which you are applying spells or presents its name: getting this wrong can mean annoyance and, possibly, instant rejection. For instance, it is Walmart not Wall Mart or Wal-Mart (which it used to be, until it rebranded in 2008); Amtrak not Amtrack; AstraZeneca not Astra-Zeneca or Astra Zeneca; PricewaterhouseCoopers not Price, Waterhouse, Coopers or PriceWaterhouseCoopers; Volkswagen not Volkswagon or VW, BBC not B.B.C. And J Sainsbury plc is the parent company of the supermarket, which now refers to itself in public as Sainsbury's – note: not Sainsburys or Sainsbury.

## Punctuation

The point of punctuation is to help the reader understand your message.

*Commas* instruct the reader to take a pause in the sentence. They are used in three ways:

**1** To break up a sentence in order to make the meaning clearer.

**2** To separate a piece of information, where they act like brackets. For instance:

– My career, military service apart, has been spent in IT.

**3** To separate items in a list. For instance:

– Expertise in Microsoft Word, PowerPoint and Excel.

Never use commas as an alternative to a full stop. It is wrong to write:

If you hold the interviews in the next two weeks I will be on holiday, I will be available after August 16th.

There should be a full stop after the word holiday.

*Colons* provide a more emphatic break in a sentence than a comma and can introduce a list separated by semi-colons. Example:

During vacations I worked in a variety of jobs: bartender; au pair to a US family; supermarket cashier; betting shop assistant.

*Apostrophes* are the biggest source of confusion. Of all the rules of punctuation they are the most frequently misused and also have the most power to infuriate any pedant who is on the receiving end of a mistake. Getting it wrong here – and this may be unfair, but there it is – is taken as a sure sign of illiteracy. So please bear in mind that *its* only ever has an apostrophe if it is short for *it is*; never in any other circumstances. Similarly, *who's* is only correct if you mean *who is*. The apostrophe here indicates a letter left out. Otherwise, apostrophes indicate possession: Jim's book, the company's shares. Where the person or object concerned is a plural – ie the word ends in *s* – you put the apostrophe after the *s*: two weeks' notice, the customers' orders (where there is more than one customer). Beware the so-called greengrocer's apostrophe – a reference to the frequency with which shops will add apostrophes to straight plurals – eg apple's, pear's. These are entirely wrong and unnecessary.

*Exclamation marks*: leave them out. People often use them to indicate light-heartedness or to try to soften a tough message. Most of such would-be humorous messages are not funny. Adding an exclamation mark does not make them funny nor does it make a potentially rude message more palatable.

*Ampersands* (the & sign): don't use them unless in a company name such as Bloggs & Bloggs plc – and only then if this is the company's own style.

## Inconsistent language in bulleted lists

When you introduce a list of bullet points, it's important to keep the internal logic consistent. Here's an example of how an admin assistant got it wrong in his CV:

My skills and experience include:

- managing anxious customers;
- invoices are processed promptly;
- have experience of all Microsoft Office applications.

The giveaway is that if you try to precede each bullet with the phrase 'My skills and experience include', you soon come to a stop. This is why it is a good idea to read your CV aloud as well as checking it on paper or on screen.

Rewritten, the list reads well because now the first word in each phrase ends in -ing:

- managing anxious customers;
- processing invoices;
- using all Microsoft Office applications.

## Other mistakes

Don't confuse *less* and *fewer* even if the world at large does. *Less* is used where there is just one of something, *fewer* where there is more than one: less cash (singular) but fewer pennies (plural). Don't say *bored of*: it's *bored by*. Never write *would of* or *must of*. The right forms are *would have* and *must have*. Don't say *lend* where you mean *borrow*. The only person who can lend something is its owner.

## Example

This is a real example. The candidate was applying for the job of chief assistant to a chief executive. What the job meant in practice was running the CEO's private office with a small team of staff whose role was providing support and advice. The candidate had already done a similar job in another organization, so he was a strong contender. But his CV was clotted with many unfortunate features. Here is a sample, with comments

> **Staff engagement**[1]: provided analysis and advice[2] to assist[3] improvement of organisational culture[4] and it's[5] impact on staff through staff participation in open access events[6] at which the CEO was present; involving other stakeholders[7] and adding stakeholder management to ensure that a wide range of opinion was canvassed and accommodated[8][9]. An on-line system for staff consultation was created[10] thus offering an effective[11] system for staff consultation, plus developing and maintaining an intranet site specifically[12] for staff comment. A network of relationships was created with senior staff enabling roleout[13] of forums for bluesky thinking[14] on how product innovation could be maximised[15][16].

[1] Unless you are an HR specialist you are unlikely to know what this phrase means.

[2] Two heavy words together.

[3] 'Help' is better than 'assist'.

[4] Meaning?

[5] No need for apostrophe here.

[6] No need for apostrophe here. What were these?

[7] Jargon words.

[8] Spelling: accommodate has two 'c's.

[9] Sentence is far too long.

[10] Passive tense.

[11] Crying out for some numbers – otherwise how do we know it was effective?

[12] Already obvious from the context.

[13] I think you mean 'rollout' but in any case this is a jargon word.

[14] Ugh. Jargon.

[15] Long-winded phrase.

[16] Whole paragraph fails to say what happened as a result: anything?

Rewritten after my stern comments and then a discussion, this was how it read:

> **Involving staff**: advised CEO on how to improve staff commitment and involvement. Developed 'Your hotline to the CEO': popular, open-invitation events attended by 500 staff across organization, in which people freely offered ideas on creating new products. Produced well-visited (25% hits of total staff in first month) online bulletin board where anyone could add further ideas. Trained heads of department in running further events across the organization to gather yet more ideas. Result: 6 successful new product lines added 2009–11 entirely from staff suggestions.

If you were on the receiving end of these paragraphs, which would you find easier to read and understand? Which would be more persuasive?

If you know this is an area of weakness for you, give your CV to someone you trust to be meticulous and well informed where language, spelling, punctuation and grammar are concerned and ask this person to comb it for potential embarrassments. Ask:

- Does it make sense to you as a total outsider?

- Is it easy to read and understand?

- What general impression of me does it give?

- What typos, misspellings, poor punctuation, misuse of words or grammatical errors can you spot?

Send off your CV only when it has passed this test.

# Endnote and references

1 Jobsworth is an entirely British term celebrated, for instance, by The Beatles in their movie *Help!* and later in the TV programme *That's Life*, which awarded Jobsworth of the Week caps to organizations which had made a particularly stupid decision based on Jobsworth principles. A Jobsworth is someone who says that it's more than their job's worth to carry out some simple task which involves making a little extra effort or being flexible about the assumed rules. Most organizations contain people who seem to know their job descriptions off by heart and refuse to do something on the

grounds that their job description does not permit them to carry out whatever the request is.

2  Oppenheimer, D M (2005) Consequences of erudite vernacular utilized irrespective of necessity: problems with using long words needlessly, *Journal of Applied Cognitive Psychology*, pp 139–56.

3  Marsh, D and Hodsdon, A (2010) *Guardian Style*, Guardian Books, London.

# BEGINNINGS AND ENDINGS

How you start and end your CV does matter and deserves a chapter to itself. Should you have an opening paragraph which sums you up, and if so, how do you write it? And when you get to the final part of the CV, should you write about your personal interests, and if so, how?

## That pesky summary paragraph

For a long time I advised clients against starting their CVs with a summary profile at the top. It can seem unnecessarily repetitive when you have a punchy first page and when your accompanying letter can make a similar statement. Also, every time I saw summary paragraphs in a draft CV I felt like cringing. Typically such paragraphs were either extremely bland and boring or positively embarrassing in the lavishness of their self-praise – and sometimes they were both. Also, they tended to pile cliché on meaningless cliché. The general result was that they all sounded exactly the same. In fact, I used to wonder if they had maybe been written in some kind of CV factory or were all pinched from the same website, but the clients all stoutly denied it.

I have come to see that these paragraphs may have a place, as long as they are written skilfully. The case for them is that because they are the first thing the reader sees they can make an instantly positive first impression. They can show the hiring manager that you have read their shortlisting criteria carefully and already possess many of the qualities and skills they are seeking. The more applications the employer is likely to receive for any one job, the more this may matter.

A profile paragraph is optional. Feel free to omit or include it as you see fit and according to the circumstances. When you are struggling to reduce the length of a CV you may feel that you can do without it. On the other hand, where your experience might otherwise seem a little thin, it can be a useful way of boosting your application.

## How not to write an opening paragraph

Katie has been running a team in a call centre and is interested in a better-paid job doing the same work for a competitor. She is a smart, sparky young woman, but how seriously would you take her as a candidate if you read this?

> Experienced, enthusiastic call centre team leader and professional running up to 20 staff in busy call centre for Direct Sales Ltd. Experienced trainer. Degree qualified.

This effort is full of the unadorned and jaded words that so many of her competitors will use: experienced, enthusiastic, professional. Other words that are popular with unthinking or naive writers of opening paragraphs are: manager, leader, team player, good communicator, reliability, strategic, challenge. These words often have added adjectives such as: outstanding, brilliant, self-motivated, well presented, disciplined.

To take just three of these words and phrases, if you are not professional and enthusiastic you might just as well not bother applying for the job. If you constantly need others to motivate you then you will be deeply unattractive as an employee: so self-motivation should be taken for granted. If the employer has asked for experience then assume all your competitors will also have experience. And a degree on its own is nothing special and is no longer a guarantee of high intelligence.

# How to write a powerful summary paragraph

Go back to the analysis of your brand and brand promise (Chapter 4). This should contain the words that express your uniqueness.

Now gut the job pack: highlight the words the employer uses in their advertisement. There will probably be up to 12 key words that describe what they are looking for. Compare these words with the words you have written in your personal brand analysis. Do they seem a good match? If yes, carry on. If no, it's not your job and don't take the application any further.

Ask yourself what problems this employer wants to have solved. How far have you solved such problems already in your career? What evidence can you offer?

## *The formula*

The heading – use any of these:

Career summary;

Profile;

Summary;

Personal profile;

None of the above; just go straight into it on the assumption that it will be obvious what its purpose is

Wherever possible, open by describing yourself by using the name of the job for which the employer is recruiting and add a brief description including your years of experience. This assumes, of course, that you really have experience in this role or in something which is recognizably similar.

The employer is looking for a medical education writer and you have worked as a journalist on a medical magazine; therefore your experience is relevant, so you open with:

Medical education writer and journalist, 3 years' experience.

Similarly, if the employer describes the job as sales assistant and you have worked in a shop where sales staff are called customer service advisors, describe yourself as sales assistant for purposes of that application. Where you are hoping to make the transition from one role to another, then bring in one of the key words associated with the new role, if you can do this without bending the truth. So, for instance, if you are a staff nurse and Registered General Nurse (RGN) hoping to progress to a ward manager role and have experience as a shift leader deputizing for a ward manager, you might begin:

> Ward shift leader, RGN, 18 months' experience deputizing for Ward Manager, leading teams of registered nurses and care assistants.

Add the context – the organization or the details of the particular environment in which you have gained your experience:

> Field chemist, 6 years' experience managing hazardous waste in nuclear energy sector.

> Traffic engineer with 4 years' post-qualification experience gained in East Anglian Local Authority, working on bus priority schemes as traffic planner.

Give tangible evidence of problems you have solved:

> Experienced site manager, successfully resolving multiple problems of communication between architects, builders and surveyors. Deal skilfully with customer complaints; track record of service recovery in challenging circumstances.

Mention any outstanding skills, attributes and knowledge you possess and which the employer has listed as essential:

> Interim manager with 12 years of chief executive experience, specializing in financial turnaround.

> Fully familiar with applications support and service management, using Net, Java, SQL and server technologies (Exchange, Windows Server) in a leading software house.

> Non-executive director with 8 years of main board retail experience.

## Avoiding wishy-washy claims

First of all there is no point in describing yourself as 'dynamic' or 'results-oriented' – two favourite words used by employers in their ads – if the rest of your CV does not support such claims. If you are truly dynamic, then you will be able to demonstrate an impressive record of fast improvements of some kind, backed up by evidence – for instance of reduction in rework rates, decreases in cycle time, better results of one kind or another. Where this is the case, then flag it in your summary paragraph:

Improved A level A* pass rates by 20% in one year.

Cut sickness absence levels from 18% to 6% over two-year period through devising and implementing new policy.

Where you make claims about other popularly sought qualities, add some words which give it more meaning. So rather than claiming you have excellent communication skills, say what the context is and what distinguishes your skills.
Examples:

Speedy drafting of clear board papers.

Chair 3–4 meetings a week with focus on speed, decisions and involvement.

Experienced conference speaker.

Careful copy editor with good eye for grammar, spelling and punctuation.

Counsellor with ability to listen without judgement to people with long-standing addiction problems.

Advocate for asylum seekers and refugees; translator with court experience.

Front desk receptionist able to make every visitor welcome.

Describe training or qualifications the employer has listed as essential and which you possess:

Fellow of Institution of Civil Engineers.

Chartered Member of Institute of Personnel and Development.

MSc in Systems Technology.

Give some flavour of how you work.
Add anything extra which is unusual and attractive, so if you have won an award, written articles, can speak another language fluently, belong to a prestigious committee, initiated something special, have

a sporting achievement which is worth boasting about, mention it, especially if it has some relevance to the job you are applying for:

Bilingual in English and German.

Won a Plain English Award in < date > for Borders Agency pamphlet on immigration law.

Won a Harkness Fellowship in < date >, spending a year in Dallas, Texas, carrying out research project on patient-centred primary care.

Have published 8 peer-reviewed research papers on the sociology of family dynamics.

Edited student newspaper *Univoice* in final year at university.

Trustee of Day-to-Day, a local charity specializing in clients with Alzheimer's disease.

Founded and am music director and conductor for 60-strong community choir.

Set up innovative tenants' management committee for housing estate in area of severe social deprivation.

Cross-Channel swimmer.

Wrote, produced and performed in play for Edinburgh Fringe in < date >.

Played hockey for Surrey between < date > and < date >.

Stick to between 35 and 70 words. Examples:

Clinical research associate; 8 years' oncology and antibody technology experience in Japan and Korea for global pharmaceutical company; 5 years' monitoring clinical trials and international site management; innovative ideas for new methodologies; enjoy working with gifted clinical specialists; PhD in Medicinal Chemistry; fluent Japanese; half-blue in Fencing.

Senior sales negotiator with 7 years' experience in leading London estate agencies; specialist in commercial property; gained significant numbers of new clients in intensely competitive market; increased lettings income by 20% over 2 years; particularly enjoy client contact and 'difficult' negotiations; renowned for bringing bounce and energy to my work. TV *Mastermind* competitor and quarter-finalist < date >.

Office manager with long track record in small and medium-sized businesses; unflappable juggler of multiple tasks including diary management for 10 consultants, credit and debt-management, stock control to minimize overspends; careful bookkeeper, deal with VAT returns; skilful liaison with accountants and other professional advisors; troubleshooter successfully solving crises with building including dealing with aftermath of a fire. Keen photographer; winner of several amateur photographer competitions.

Katie could improve her summary statement in similar vein. The potential employer has identified the skills and experience they want. These include: constant improvement in efficiency; management skills such as ability to motivate and inspire and thus to retain talented staff; preparing and running reports using Customer Relations Management (CRM) software; training; staff-scheduling experience and preparing budgetary reports. Katie knows, because she has done her private research, that the company has recently lost market share, partly because of the poor quality of its call centre staff, many of whom have recently lost their jobs and been replaced by more carefully recruited people with higher levels of aptitude. So she expects, if appointed, to have to deal with low morale, confusion and a team consisting of a mix of old and new staff. She also knows that the company is cutting back on employing external trainers in order to save money. Katie likes the sector she works in, is undaunted by its challenges, especially those of motivating staff, many of whom, she knows, see the work as 'just a job' and, if not well managed, are inclined to resign after only a short period in the job or to take unauthorized 'sickies'. Much of this she will be able to spell out later in the CV, but she rewords her profile paragraph like this:

Call centre team leader, 4 years' experience in pressured sales environment, devising rotas, managing budgets; twice won Team Leader of the Year award, fully able to use CRM software. Improved team attendance records reducing sickness absence from 15% to 7%. Redesigned 'Handling difficult customers' and 'Telephone skills' courses, personally training 100+ staff. Enjoy challenges of motivating teams to improve response times, balancing business with customer needs; proud of creating enjoyable, productive climate for staff.

Something like this is far more likely to engage the reader – and, in fact, the actual client on whom this example is based went on to be shortlisted, did a triumphantly successful interview and was offered the job. The new employers rightly considered themselves lucky to have attracted her.

# 'Career objective' statements

Like the summary paragraph, there are mixed views on whether it is sensible to write a statement of your career objective. These statements are more common in the USA and much rarer in the UK. The case for them is that they can be helpful when you are at the beginning of your career, for instance as a school leaver or new graduate and do not have much work experience. In these circumstances it can suggest strong motivation and clarity about why you want the job or why you want to work for a particular employer.

Examples:

> Having just left school with 3 good A levels, I am seeking a job in accountancy with the aim of qualifying as an accountancy technician by the time I am 23.

> Media Studies graduate (2.1) looking for first role in arts administration where my passion for performance arts and ability as an organizer can be put to good use.

These statements can also be helpful when you are hoping to make a transition from one type of career to another, one sector to another or where your experience does not seem like an obviously good fit with what the employer has specified.

Examples:

> E-commerce web developer now wishing to make the transition to a marketing role in online sales.

> Human resources manager, CIPD, with substantial training experience looking to make a move into full-time management training.

Note that in careers where there is a typical progression from early-career jobs to other types of role, there is no need for the career objective statement as recruiters will take your motivation for granted to some extent.

If you have had a career break or been a full-time parent/carer then it can be useful to emphasize your determination to get back into employment, and this is one place where using the first person (I/me) is acceptable:

> After a period of 8 years as full-time parent, I am now keen to re-establish my career in retail banking and am looking for a part-time job as a quantitative analyst.

> Having just returned from a year-long period travelling the world, I intend refocusing my career on opportunities in environmental consultancy.

## Combining the two

Sometimes there is a case for combining the summary paragraph with the career objective. This can work where your experience is a reasonably good but not a perfect fit with what the employer is looking for. Here you simply add the career objective as the final sentence of your summary emphasizing your motivation:

> Accredited forensic accountant and expert witness; developed computerized applications to analyse evidence of fraud. Manage hard-working team of 12. Now seeking to move to local authority sector as director of finance with strategic responsibility for financial health of whole organization.

# The 'Personal interests' paragraph

Having decided whether you want to have a summary profile at the start of the CV, you also have to decide whether to add a personal interests paragraph. Opinions are divided about whether you should include this or not. I favour it because it shows that you are a whole human being and not a work robot. However, take care with what you say. I have seen many hundreds of CVs where the authors describe the following as their interests:

> My family and friends; cooking; reading; walking; most sports; travel, films and theatre.

There are several problems with this kind of list. First, most people could lay claim to them. We all have families and friends. Most people can do at least a little cooking; everyone does some walking and has seen films or gone to the theatre, even if the last theatre visit was many years ago to see *The Mousetrap*. This kind of list does nothing to differentiate you – one of the main purposes of a CV. Second, some candidates want to make themselves seem cultured and special by laying claim to hobbies or interests that they believe will impress the reader but which they do not in fact have. At interview I have seen candidates who claim 'theatre' as one of their interests have their bluff called when they are asked 'What was the last play you saw?' or 'What kind of theatre do you like?' and then fumble embarrassedly for an answer. If something isn't really one of your interests, don't claim it. Other mistakes people make here are to claim so many hobbies that the employer will wonder how they ever have time for work: this, too, is unrealistic. Most of us only truly have three or four interests which occupy substantial slabs of our attention. If you say you like reading, then say what kind of reading: for instance, historical accounts of 20th-century events; sports hero biographies; modern US fiction; Victorian classics; Man Booker-style bestsellers. If you like movies, then it's better to say what type appeals to you. No one likes 'every' kind of film, so state the genre that attracts you: sci-fi, romantic comedies, Argentinean indie, post-war British thrillers – and there's no shame whatsoever in admitting to a liking for Hollywood blockbusters. If you really do love cooking or DIY and are a bit of an expert, then say so and describe your expertise.

Attention-grabbing interests that I have enjoyed reading include all of these, given just as the candidates wrote them:

Member of the UK Wolf Conservation Trust and enjoy taking them for walks.

Collector of British commemorative china from 1920s onwards.

Competitive dingy racing on Norfolk Broads.

Getting my golf handicap down.

Amateur actor and member of village drama society.

Enthusiastic reader of modern detective fiction; devoted fan of Elmore Leonard, Val McDermid and Ian Rankin.

Restorer of classic cars and enjoy attending rallies with other enthusiasts and maniacs.

Mountain climber: entered the British Three Peaks Challenge in 2011.

Dedicated member of < name > Operatic Society, in which I sing soprano and have recently been promoted to principal roles.

Breed and show Abyssinian cats; occasionally produce a champion.

At weekends I can often be found running around central Manchester or dangling from an indoor climbing wall.

Making birthday cakes and hand-crafted greetings cards.

Whatever your interests, keep the list to no more than four lines, though three is better. The employer does not want a full account of how you spend every moment of your leisure. Occasionally I meet a client who gloomily tells me that he (it is usually he) does not have any hobbies or interests other than work. Probing reveals that this is substantially true. If this is how it is for you, then just omit the whole section. Some types of employer actually like the idea that they employ work machines and if this is the case, then the omission will be met with approval.

| CHECKLIST ON DESCRIBING PERSONAL INTERESTS | | |
|---|---|---|
| | Yes | No |
| Do these interests help me stand out? | | |
| Have I been specific in describing them? | | |
| Are they genuinely what interests me? | | |
| If asked at interview, will I be able to say more and with enthusiasm? | | |

# FORMAT IS EVERYTHING

In writing your CV you have a number of choices and this chapter looks at what the main choices are and how to make a sensible decision about which will suit you best. In practice you may want to create CVs using several of these formats, depending on circumstances and the job for which you are bidding.

## The chronological CV

This one is the classic: the most familiar and also the easiest to create. It is an historical account of your career, starting with the most recent job and working backwards in time.

There are many advantages to writing your CV this way. It is the one most familiar to recruiters and is simple for a reader to absorb because it shows your career path in an easily followed progression. It is particularly suitable for people whose careers have taken interesting swerves from one organization or sector to another, or who have had rapid promotion. Where your career has enabled you to develop specialist expertise, it is simple for a reader to see exactly how this has happened because it stresses continuity and also makes it obvious why you might be bidding for promotion or a change of scene as your next logical step. It is possible to show steadiness and persistence through a career history of this sort, and this can appeal to employers. Demonstrating promotions and impressive job titles can also help a future employer understand that you have much to offer.

However, there are disadvantages to this format. Where you have been in one organization for a long time it can sometimes be challenging to make it clear that you have had a number of different jobs and roles: the impression might be that you have hung around in one place far too long, suggesting timidity or a career that has become moribund. This is especially true if you have essentially been doing the same job for lengthy periods, even if the label 'senior' (eg senior team leader, senior producer, senior accountant, senior analyst) has been added to your job title as a reward for the length of your service and to justify some extra pay. The exception might be where your previous or present employer is a household name, such as a large bank or insurance company, or an apparently 'glamorous' employer such as a theatre or broadcasting organization. Where this is the case, people may more readily understand the appeal of staying in it for many years.

When you have had breaks in employment because of illness or raising children, such breaks are immediately obvious from this type of CV. It is also harder to demonstrate transferable skills with this format, so it is not always useful for people leaving a career where long service is the norm – for instance, the uniformed services, medicine or higher education. Job titles in a long-stay organization may not have any resemblance to the title of the job for which you are bidding, so this is also a disadvantage. For school leavers and young graduates, the chronological CV is not usually the best way to present yourself as it spotlights the thinness of your experience, however much you make of your qualifications, temporary roles or vacation jobs.

This CV will normally take up between one and two pages. The ideal layout will have your contact details and most recent jobs on page 1 and the rest of your career history on page 2, then your qualifications and personal interests.

*Your name*
*House name or number; street name*
*City/town/county, postcode*
*Mobile number     Home number     E-mail*

*SUMMARY*

One paragraph (see page 99)

*CAREER HISTORY AND ACHIEVEMENTS*[1]

*Dates* [from when to present]
*Most recent job title, name of employer*

Two lines on the nature of your responsibilities: eg purpose of the organization or your department; number of people you managed or worked with; what you were accountable for in numbers (budget, turnover, other targets) contacts with customers/clients.

- One major achievement and how you accomplished it (see page 85).
- A second major achievement.
- A third major achievement.
- A fourth major achievement.

*Dates* [from when to when]
*Job before present one, job title, name of employer*
As above but only three bullet points.

*Dates* [from when to when]
As above but even briefer.

*Earlier career: summary*
A list of dates, job titles and employers, with no further details.

*QUALIFICATIONS* [most recent first]

| | | |
|---|---|---|
| Date | Name of qualification | Name of awarding body |
| Date | Name of qualification | Name of awarding body |

*TRAINING AND PERSONAL DEVELOPMENT* [2]

| | | |
|---|---|---|
| Date | Name of course or event | Brief account of its focus and purpose and what you learnt from it. |

*FURTHER INFORMATION*

This could include memberships of professional organizations and accreditations; any community activity in which you play a significant role; committee memberships; conferences at which you have spoken; publications [3].

*PERSONAL INTERESTS*

2 lines.

---

[1] Alternative titles here could include:

Career review
Job history
Career and accomplishments
Employment history

[2] Only include anything here if the course has prestige or was important in your personal development (see pages 71–72).

[3] Any of these could form a heading of its own if it makes a good match to the job you are applying for.

# The skills/competency-based CV

This version of the CV takes longer to write and is especially worth doing if you are prepared to invest time in researching the employer and what they want. With a skills-based CV you can demonstrate how close a match you are to what the employer seeks.

This format is worth considering when you are aiming to change sectors or careers, because in effect you are showing that your skills are transferable. It is often the best format to use when it is clear that the employer has done a careful analysis of the skills the job needs and has listed them as competencies (page 67). When this is the case, you should take each skill or competency area one by one in the same order as they are listed by the employer, as this is often an order of priority in the employer's mind. This makes it easy to shortlist you because in effect you are doing the recruiter's job for them: 'So you say you want a skilled team leader? Yes! That's me: see how closely my experience matches what you want!'

Whereas the chronological CV shows your history, the skills-based CV invites the reader to look at the future. It is also a good bet for young people without much of a career to describe and for people who have had a spell at home as a parent or carer, as you can depict the skills you have acquired in an unpaid capacity. Where there are jobs in your employment history that do not seem a perfect fit with the job for which you are applying, this format helps you soften their impact. Gaps will still be visible because you will be listing your career history as well, but they may seem less important.

One disadvantage of this format is that you will be recrafting at least some of it every single time you apply for a job, but that is something that probably should happen with the chronological CV as well. Some employers say they prefer the chronological format because it allows them to see more clearly where you have acquired the skills you claim and may be suspicious of a format which allows you to bury embarrassments more easily.

*Your name*
*House name or number; street name*
*City/town/county, postcode*
*Mobile number     Home number     E-mail*

*SUMMARY*

One paragraph (see page 99).

*SKILLS AND ACHIEVEMENTS*

- Skill or competency 1

- Skill or competency 2

- Skill or competency 3

- Skill or competency 4

- Skill or competency 5

- Skill or competency 6

- Skill or competency 7

- Skill or competency 8

This should take up page 1.

*CAREER HISTORY* [backwards from present]

**Date – date**      **Job title**      **Employer**
One line on accountabilities.

**Date to date**      **Job title**      **Employer**
One line on accountabilities.

**Date – date**      **Job title**      **Employer**
One line on accountabilities.

Then list earlier career with dates, job titles and employer without describing the accountabilities.

*QUALIFICATIONS* [most recent first]

| Date | Name of qualification | Name of awarding body |
|---|---|---|
| Date | Name of qualification | Name of awarding body |
| Date | Name of qualification | Name of awarding body |

*TRAINING AND PERSONAL DEVELOPMENT*[2]

| Date | Name of course or event | Brief account of its focus and purpose and what you learnt from it. |
|---|---|---|

*FURTHER INFORMATION*

This could include memberships of professional organizations and accreditations; any community activity in which you play a significant role; committee memberships, conferences at which you have spoken; publications[3].

*PERSONAL INTERESTS*

2 lines

---

[1] The circumstances, the problems, how you solved them; what the tangible end result was (see page 83 for more on how to write this). Aim for about 6 lines for each bullet.

[2] Only include anything here if the course has prestige or was important in your personal development (see page 71).

[3] Any of these could form a heading of its own if it makes a good match to the job you are applying for.

# The hybrid

The hybrid, which mates the chronological with the skills-based CV, allows you to have the best of both worlds. This makes it a good choice for many people. It works well for mature jobseekers and career changers because it allows you to describe your skills and/or accomplishments as well as offering a chronological context. It is not usually so suitable for people at the beginnings of their careers and may not work so well for people with substantial career gaps or long periods of unemployment. In the hybrid, you list your jobs chronologically but point to skills and attainments under each job, putting most emphasis on the current or last job.

*Your name*
*House name or number; street name*
*City/town/county, postcode*
*Mobile number    Home number    E-mail*

*PROFILE*

One paragraph (see page 99).

*SUMMARY OF SKILLS AND ACCOMPLISHMENTS*

Aim to choose about 3 each from technical or knowledge-based skills or accomplishments, eg unusual or in-depth qualifications; anything that builds on personal reputation and recognition in your sector; feedback from colleagues; specialized licensing or expertise; 'soft' skills (such as influencing, negotiating) and skills that are really qualities such as personal resilience, commitment to development.

- Skill or accomplishment 1: one or two lines for each skill.

- Skill 2

- Skill 3

- Skill 4

- Skill 5

- Skill 6

- Skill 7

*EXPERIENCE AND ACHIEVEMENTS*

*Dates* [from when to present]
*Most recent job title, name of employer*
Two bullet-pointed achievements that support your claims to the skills above.

*Dates* [from when to when] *Previous job, title, name of employer*
As above.

*Dates* [from when to when] *Job before that, title, name of employer*
As above but only one bullet point.

*PREVIOUS CAREER*

Summary of dates, job titles and employers.

*EDUCATION, TRAINING AND QUALIFICATIONS*

*PERSONAL INTERESTS*

# The one-page CV

The convention with CVs is that two pages is the ideal length. However, there are times when a one-pager is needed. Typically this is when a headhunter or recruiter wants to see at a glance what you have to offer in order to put you forward to an employer. If interested in you, they will ask for a fuller CV later and may also advise you on which format will be best. The one-page CV can also be useful where you are approaching a recruiter yourself, where in effect it is a calling card, to be followed later by a fuller version. My clients often complain bitterly about having to reduce their lives to one page, but if it is asked for, then you need to know how to do it. Ruthless editing is essential. You are picking the absolute highlights of your career, ideally the ones that have the strongest link to the skills and qualities that the possible new job needs.

*Your name*
*House name or number, street name*
*City, town village name, postcode*

## SUMMARY PARAGRAPH
5 lines maximum.

## SKILLS AND ACCOMPLISHMENTS
8 bullet points covering your years of experience in the sector; reputation; publications if any; specialized expertise; major accomplishments – the difference you have made in various jobs; 'soft' skills.

## CAREER HISTORY
Starting with the most recent and working backwards. a list of jobs with dates, job titles, name of employer and major responsibilities.

## QUALIFICATIONS WITH DATES, AWARDING BODY

# Medical CVs

Although the general rule for CVs is no more than two pages, there are exceptions and the medical profession is one of them. The permission to use more pages probably arises from concern about quality and standards. Medical selectors need to see a full career history and to have a comprehensive view of what a doctor can do. A decent CV is even more important for doctors than it used to be, given that the number of training and consultant posts is shrinking and that competition for general practitioner posts is keen. Unlike other types of CV, qualifications go on the first page as medicine is a qualification-led profession with a strong respect for academic achievement, and your qualification history gives the reader a quick overview of who you are and where you are in your career. The CV needs to give GMC and Medical Defence Union details plus fuller details of earlier career than is usual in other types of CV and if there are gaps, you should explain them. Referees are normally omitted from other CVs but they are important in medical CVs as they show which senior colleagues are willing to endorse you. The grander and better known your referees, the better it is for you. Any referee needs to know which job you are applying for and to give their permission in writing.

In terms of length, general principles are:

Junior doctors: 3–5 pages;

Mid career: 5–9 pages;

Transition to consultant: 9–12 pages;

Consultants: 9–16 pages.

In all other respects, the same rules apply as for other CVs – for instance, giving examples of problems you can solve, writing clearly and simply, creating an attractive layout.

*Your name*
*Address and postcode*
*Mobile and home landline numbers*

*CAREER SUMMARY* (optional – see page 99).
Career objective: describe in no more than 3 lines which direction you want to take and why. Be specific – eg about which particular branch of orthopaedics you want to specialize in or what kind of general practice you wish to join and what you can offer.

*GMC STATUS:* full registration numbers and National Training Number.

*MEDICAL DEFENCE UNION:* registration numbers.

*QUALIFICATIONS.*

These should include A levels as well as higher education qualifications. Start with the most recent and work backwards.

| Dates | Institution | Name and level of qualification |
|---|---|---|
|  |  |  |

Give details of any prizes or special awards, grants, scholarships or fellowships.

*EMPLOYMENT HISTORY* (starting with the most recent and working backwards).

| Dates | Name of employer | Grade and speciality | Name of supervising consultant |
|---|---|---|---|
|  |  |  |  |

Give highlights of each post, emphasizing what you learnt and how you applied it.

*SKILLS AND PROFICIENCIES.*
(List as full bullet point list of procedures – eg diagnostic – and skills you are confident of using.)

*TEACHING EXPERIENCE*

*RESEARCH EXPERIENCE*

*CONTINUING PROFESSIONAL DEVELOPMENT:* courses attended in the last 2 years.

*AUDITS*

*PUBLICATIONS* (the protocol is to list books first, then papers in journals and then conference papers), listing fellow authors if applicable, with full details of publisher, date, title, volume and and page numbers.

*CONFERENCE PRESENTATIONS*

*MANAGEMENT EXPERIENCE*

*PERSONAL INTERESTS*

*REFEREES*    (normally you would give three with their full academic and professional qualifications, plus their contact details, as agreed with them).

*IF YOU TRAINED OUTSIDE THE UK*
Give priority to your UK work. Include details of the International Language Testing System and the Professional Linguistic Assessment and describe your immigration status. Add any brief explanations of qualifications or experience that you think a UK employer might find hard to decode.

# Academic CVs

Academic CVs are another exception to the general rules of CV writing. They resemble medical CVs in their emphasis on qualifications, teaching and research.

Length:

Young graduate looking for research or teaching assistant role: 2–4 pages;

Mid career: 3–6 pages;

Seniors: 4–9 pages.

*Name*
*Address*
*Postcode*

*QUALIFICATIONS SUMMARY*

An overview of your formal qualifications and awards;

The number of years you have spent in areas related to the job for which you are applying;

A summary of the skills and experience you bring to the role;

A summary of personal qualities that the employer has stated they want and which you have;

A summary of achievements in the field directly relevant to the role;

A summary of contributions you have made to your field – eg research and teaching.

*EDUCATION*

Degrees – starting with PhD. Give a paragraph summary of dissertation then supervisor, dates of study, awarding body.

Earlier degree(s). Dates, awarding body and name of degree. Give details of modules and subjects if you are in early career. A brief summary is better for seniors.

Awards, scholarships, fellowships, prizes, feedback from students and other scores.

Memberships of professional bodies.

Other courses taken including any that do not have qualifications attached.

*RESEARCH*

List any not covered by PhD thesis.

*TEACHING*

| Role | Institution | Subjects taught |
|------|-------------|-----------------|

Summary of teaching skills.

Two examples of approaches and techniques that you can employ with confidence – eg facilitating problem-based learning, conducting seminars with large groups.

*PUBLICATIONS*

List full details of books and papers: publisher, co-authors, journal, volume number, title of paper, page references.

Conference speaking. List the four most recent conference appearances with details of topics and themes if you are a seasoned speaker, offering a full list on request.

Media appearances. List any contributions to TV, radio, internet.

*REFEREES*

As with medical referees, the more famous and well regarded your referees, the better this will look for you, especially if they work in the field to which you are applying. As with any referees, you must get their permission and send them the job specification.

# Teaching CVs

CVs for teachers are more like conventional CVs than academic CVs (ie for jobs in higher education). Although two pages is still the desirable length, it is more acceptable for them to stretch to three than in other professions. There are three areas you should add:

1 Further training and development are highly regarded in teaching, so you should list all courses you have attended over the last two–three years and include any that involve extensive time commitment.

2 Give details of any extra-curricular activities you have run in your present and past schools. Willingness to take a full part in the life of the school is something that all sensible head teachers seek.

3 Stress your familiarity and skill with IT, especially any skills that involve developing or using technology to deliver learning content or to manage attendance and other records.

# The biographical CV

This is not really a CV at all in the conventional sense as it lacks dates and complete employment history and usually omits full qualifications details. In essence it is a few paragraphs of advertising copy where the product is you. It is often what is required when you are a freelancer, a consultant or a performer such as an actor. The employer may say 'Send me a CV,' but the more casual and short term the period of prospective employment, the less likely it is that the employer needs to see any of the CV formats I have described in this chapter so far. A biographical CV is useful in any of these circumstances:

- as part of the home page on your personal website;

- when you are part of a team of freelancers bidding for work that is being tendered and you have each been asked to 'attach a CV';

- as back-up to any proposal you are making for freelance work;

- as the basis of a verbal script that you use to describe yourself in person to a potential employer.

The format is helpful for anyone who works freelance – for instance, graphic designers, consultants, camera crew, hairdressers, bookkeepers.

## How to write the biographical CV

Go back once more to your personal brand analysis for key words that you should include (Chapter 4). This will give you a starting point. As in every other type of CV, the tone should be confident without seeming boastful.

As a way of prompting your thinking, ask yourself:

For paragraph 1: What phrase do I need to use to describe myself in the opening sentence? Normally this will be:

- X < your name > is a < name of your job title in your branch of the profession > with < number of > years of experience in < brief description of your typical activity >.

- Who are my typical clients – or sometimes – who would I like them to be? You can define them by age, need, sector, profession, role, level of seniority or geography or some combination of all of these.

- What do these clients say to themselves about the problems that they have?

- How do my services solve these problems?

For paragraph 2: Which parts of my past career will impress these clients? What can I say about jobs I have held which will give me credibility? Note that here there is no need to give a complete list or even to state the actual names of the roles nor the dates or number of years that you worked for these organizations.

For paragraph 3: Which clients have I already worked for as a freelancer? If appropriate, add a description of the projects you have undertaken, bearing in mind that you may need to preserve client confidentiality here.

For paragraph 4: What other information can I offer about myself which fits the kind of person the client needs? This might include anything which may have put you in the public domain and which is flattering to your brand: appearances in the media, books, articles, achievements, honours, prizes (see page 107 for the section on personal information in conventional CVs for some advice and ideas here). Include a few details of your family circumstances if you like. Where you believe that qualifications will impress a reader, then add them, but again, there is no need to give details of dates and awarding bodies unless you think they are especially impressive. If the hiring employer or client wants this information then they would have asked you for a conventional CV.

Here is an example of how the format works out in practice. It is a composite created from the CVs of several executive coaches – people who operate in my own world. Note that it is written in the third person – as if it has been written about Adriana by someone else – though of course she will have written it herself:

Adriana Sample has been working as an executive coach for 7 years, coaching senior executives at director and chief executive level in organizations ranging from investment banks and insurance companies to the National Health Service. Adriana works with clients who want to become even more effective as leaders – for instance, by improving their capacity to manage stress, motivate their teams, increase their personal impact and still have a satisfying private life. She is also adept at helping people understand what makes them – and others – tick. She enjoys working with clients who are up for taking a risk and also for asking themselves, 'What next in my life?' as well as those who may have lost a little confidence in themselves and their skills, perhaps because of recent changes in their lives and careers.

Adriana has extensive experience as a leader herself, and before becoming a coach held senior civil service roles at the Treasury and Cabinet Office where she led major programmes of transformation to increase efficiency. Prior to that she worked for telecoms company Timpani as director of organizational development. She has personal knowledge of the pain and upheaval that change can bring to the people you manage, as well as many years of introducing innovation in earlier career which included a period as a senior HR professional at Debenhams plc and a graduate traineeship at Marks & Spencer.

Her current clients include many household-name organizations such as NatWest Bank, Costa Coffee, the Arcadia Group, the General Medical Council, the University of London, The John Lewis Partnership, KPMG, and NHS organizations of all types.

Adriana holds a BSc in Psychology, an MBA from the University of Bradford, and is an EMCC-accredited Master Practitioner in coaching.

She is a parent-governor for her local academy and a trustee member of the Age Concern Board in the London Borough of XX. She is married and has two grown-up children.

Adriana's biographical CV works well because it clearly describes her professional identity and her target market: senior managers. It identifies the typical problems that they have – for instance, being overwhelmed by the stress of their work and lacking confidence or losing their way in their careers. It is written in plain English and gives some hints about what motivates her as a coach – for instance, her curiosity about what makes people tick. The second paragraph picks out highlights from her career without being a complete account of it. It is meant to emphasize that she understands the corporate environment because she has worked in it herself in senior roles, though you should note that the word 'senior' has no exact meaning and can be stretched to cover any number of jobs. The third paragraph names her most easily recognizable clients and is meant to reassure a potential buyer that other impressive organizations have hired her, but note that it does not say how many such clients she has worked with in any of the organizations – it could be one or it could be hundreds. The final paragraph is meant to convey that she is a coach who has invested seriously in her own development. She may have other qualifications, but these are the ones she thinks will persuade people to take her on as a coach. Mentioning her charity work and her children suggests that she is a mature, sensible, community-minded person.

# SPECIAL ADDITIONS

It all depends on the circumstances, but there can be a number of other tactics and additions that you might consider using to boost your chances of catching the eye of a potential employer. This chapter introduces you to some of the most valuable.

## A personal website

When you are embarked on a freelance career, a personal website is a must. It is not the place where people will actually make the decision to work with you but it may well be an introduction or follow-up to a face-to-face meeting, like every other type of online activity. A website need not be elaborate; depending on the nature of your business, four pages might be ample: a home page which describes what you do and who your typical customers are, some customer testimonials, a sample of your work and a Contact-me page which generates an automatic e-mail. Mostly a personal website will be visited by people who have already heard of you and are checking you out. If they like the look of what they see, they will follow this up with an e-mail or phone call. A personal website is really there to give people an idea of what it would be like working with you, just as a CV does, but the website is more informal. A website tells employers and potential clients what kinds of problems you can solve for them and allows you to use graphics, including a photograph of yourself. Choose a proper domain name – ideally some version of your own name – and keep the address short, memorable, simple and easy to spell. Bear in mind that, 80 per cent of the time, people only read the home page, so this is the one to concentrate on. A computer screen is landscape shaped rather than portrait shaped, so design and write the copy so that it reads easily and clearly this way. Short, punchy copy is better than long words and sentences, so think *Daily Mirror* rather than *Financial Times*. It should be typo free and if you have included links to other sites, make sure they work.

Your home page is, once more, where the work you do on your personal brand (Chapter 4) will pay dividends. It should say everything that is unique and positive about what you can offer. One word of warning: a personal website is not just your CV regurgitated; it is a different way of promoting yourself with different language and appearance. Once you have the site established, you might consider adding articles and updating them every six weeks or so, details about articles or books you have written and links to other sites such as your LinkedIn page or to affinity groups of which you are a member. If you have given a presentation which has been videoed, and which you believe is a good advertisement for what you offer, then you may be able to negotiate a link to whichever site is hosting it. This client made good use of this idea:

> I was applying for a job in higher education and wanted to show what I could do as a teacher. When I was asked to give a workshop at a conference, I arranged for a friend who knows about these things to come along with a video camera and to capture the opening phase and then a few snatches of the workshop activity. It went well. We did some very simple editing to get it down to about eight minutes altogether. I put it on my own website and also uploaded it to YouTube. In making my application I put the links on my electronically presented CV. At the interview I was praised for my 'enterprise' and the panel chair said she had watched it. I'm sure that was one of the reasons I got the job because it was clear I'd gone to a lot of trouble, also that I was proud of my work and of course they could actually see a sample of it to back up what I claimed.

A website is an excellent addition to a conventional CV for people whose work is in areas where you will need to demonstrate a portfolio at some point. So for architects, designers, artists, actors, singers and others in professions where people choose you on the basis of demonstrated talent and flair, it can be essential to offer a potential employer the chance to click through an electronically presented portfolio. In fact, some websites are merely another way of hosting a portfolio. At interview stage you may even be asked to present a slideshow of your work rather than bringing along an actual portfolio as was traditional. Well-lit, beautifully framed digital photography is obviously a must here, but if you are in this field you will already be well aware of that.

## First person or third person?

A website is more convincing if it is written in the third person – that is, as if some genial fan has written the copy. For examples of how this works, look at the author's biography on the cover of any book. It would be rare for the publishers to write this but is always written as if they have. Some people don't like the artifice involved in pretending that someone else has written the copy and they unashamedly use the first person. It's up to you. Whichever 'person' you use, beware of over-the-top glowing self-praise. Avoid using phrases such as 'outstanding leader', 'consummate professional' or 'especially talented x or y'. It looks naive and most readers will dismiss it as puffery anyway.

You can buy, or download free, software which allows you to construct a website yourself, but unless you are a professional graphic designer, this is virtually always a job better delegated to someone else – but not to your nerdy nephew who offers to do it for free. Where this happens it usually ends in tears with deadlines missed, dodgy quality and the nephew or his proud parent departing in a huff, leaving the website commissioner having to start all over again, this time with someone who is going to be paid on a fully professional basis.

## Pluses

A personal website can work for these reasons:

- It allows for more creativity.
- It can be longer than a conventional CV.
- You can showcase your work through photographs, video or links to articles and books.

- For people who are looking for freelance employment, it is a must.

- You can make easy links to and from Facebook or LinkedIn pages and, indeed, can put the link on your paper or standard CV for employers to take up if they wish.

## *Minuses*

There are some disadvantages:

- Employers repeatedly say that they do not want to see elaborate CVs with fancy graphics, and a personal website is, in effect, just that – but, of course, it is their choice whether they go to the site or not.

- Where you commission someone else to build you the site, it will involve a significant investment of money.

- If you do it yourself, it will take a large amount of time and effort.

- A website must be regularly maintained and updated.

# Blogs

A blog is an alternative to or an extra feature on a personal website. It can work well – as long as you are clear what it is for and who can read it. The same cautions apply here as to social networking sites (page 32). If your blog contains indiscretions about your personal life or your current employer and colleagues, then it will be a hindrance, not a help, in the process of finding a new job. You may need to think carefully about your own privacy, giving yourself a blog name which will protect your identity, but be aware that it is likely you will give many clues which would enable a diligent sleuth to work out who you are. For instance, if you say you work at 'a government office in Cardiff as a middle manager' and also mention that you have a Westie dog, identifying you could be pretty easy. Don't use pseudonyms that look or sound like your real name, so real name Angela, blog name Angel 1, would give instant clues. If you are in a job but looking for a new one, don't blog at work: companies understandably object to employees using company time and resources for private concerns. The whole point of creating a job-search blog is for people to contact you, so make sure that this is easy while also protecting yourself from unwanted attention.

Sparklingly good prose is essential. Blogs should be free from spelling errors and typos and the tone should be measured. Researching this section, the majority of the blogs I read did not, alas, meet this standard. Most were guilty of all the familiar errors: apostrophes in the wrong places, confusing the spelling of words that sound the same but have different meanings and spellings, writing everything in lower case so I appears as i, adding multiple exclamation marks, a frenzied tone – and many more of the common affronts to good writing.

Two kinds of blog can help:

*An account of your job search.* There have been some good examples here of people who write vividly and record their progress, frustrations, hopes and fears as they search for a new job. A successful blog of this kind is really a way of showing once more what kind of a colleague you would make, what you offer and how you cope with disappointment and stress. The tone should be stoical humour and patience. It never works if the blog seems ranting and strident, or names individuals whom the blogger considers are viciously or stupidly standing in their way. Swearing, racist, sexist or ageist comments will of course ensure that any sensible employer avoids you.

*A series of think pieces about your sector or profession.* This is more useful. In effect you are working on the border between journalism and an informal telephone conversation that you might have with a friend. The purpose of this kind of blog is to establish you as a thoughtful, industrious person with good ideas. The right tone is essential: avoid anything that could come across as hysterical, whining, spiteful or angry. Use the first person so that you establish an intimate tone and address the reader as 'you', but beware of over-disclosing. Ask yourself, 'How will this strike a potential boss? What am I betraying about myself that could seem a little embarrassing if I read it in a year's time?' Draft the blog and then leave it for a few hours, read it again, make sensible edits and only then post it.

Successful blogs of this type could be commentary on any of the following:

● global, national or local trends;

● descriptions of specific incidents which shed light on current topics of concern in your field;

- analysis of what makes relationships work in your area – for instance, between customers and staff, staff and bosses;

- how to make a business more customer centred;

- making improvements that would also cut costs;

- how to avoid waste and rework;

- tools, techniques and tips of all sorts; for instance, how to manage stress in the workplace, how to prioritize your work, get enough rest and play in your life, deal with poorly performing colleagues.

## For and against blogging

There is a strong case for blogging. It shows energy and commitment and can convey your personality more intensely than the typical CV can. It can create interest if you do it well, in addition to being a showcase for your professional expertise. The case against blogging is that it can be difficult to conceal your identity and the temptation to be indiscreet can be overwhelming; it may say more about you and in undesirable ways than you realize. Also, it can betray lack of skill in writing.

# A special report for the employer

Some US books on bidding for a job recommend that along with your CV or application, you offer an unsolicited unique report to the potential employer outlining how you would do the job or analysing their problems with your own suggested solutions. The theory is that you show your enterprise, demonstrate the amount of research you have done and the quality of your thinking. All these are excellent aims. There is indeed a case for the special report but only in certain circumstances.

I do not recommend that you do this where you are an external candidate. However wonderful and thorough your research into the organization and the job, you are an outsider with an outsider's perspective and your analysis is likely to be partial and incomplete. You do not have full access to what is actually going on inside and are unlikely to understand all the sensitivities involved. You do not have the employer's permission to offer your report and therefore run a severe risk of alienating the reader by appearing impertinent or tactless. This is because even the most saintly boss is likely to be part of whatever the problems are and will not relish hearing all about them from a complete stranger. This applies even where what you say is spot on – in fact, it probably applies even more strongly when you are completely correct in your conclusions. The only exception to this rule is where you are specifically requested to submit a report along these lines. This is sometimes the case for the most senior managerial jobs where candidates are invited to write what is in effect a personal manifesto outlining how they would do the job.

However, when you are already an insider and are applying for promotion, there is a much stronger case for adding a document of this kind. You will know the politics, you have experienced the issues at first hand, you want to show that you have a taste for improving and strengthening the product or service in which you would be involved. The more simple and low cost your suggested solutions are – ie they do not involve hiring more people or spending more money – the better they are likely to be received. The tone still needs care: you are aiming for something judicious, friendly, professional and fair.

## The format for a special report

Overall length: two A4 pages maximum because no one has time to read more than this, and keeping it brief will force you to concentrate on the main points. The structure should be:

1 Introduction. One paragraph. Says what your topic is, why you are writing the report and who it is for.

2 Describe how you gathered evidence and how reliable such evidence is. For instance, if you have relied solely on statistics, what about the human element? If your evidence is purely anecdotal, then own up to its limitations.

3 The problems. Make a bulleted list of problems, setting out what makes them problems and what could happen if they are not solved.

4 The possible solutions. Deal with each of the problems in the same order, suggesting how they might be solved.

5 Recommendations. Your suggestions for immediate action.

## *Alternatives*

Rather than writing something specific to the employer, you might want to consider creating an intriguing and useful general article which is likely to interest any employer in the sector in which you are aiming to work. All employers are interested in how they might improve financial results, decrease waste, increase staff satisfaction, please regulators, attract more customer loyalty, and so on. Learn from advertisers here: they have found out what attracts our attention in terms of words:

Special offer: using numbers: eg 6 ways to save money.

New: implying urgency; limited time to ...

Fresh: how to ...

Simple: practical.

Save (money/time): secret; for instance, 10 secrets of ...

Examples:

A candidate applying for a job in higher education offered a one-page document headed '10 successful ways to recruit students from China'.

A management consultant concocted a list of simple tips, all culled from well-known books and websites, about how to retain client loyalty in a severe recession.

A senior NHS nurse-manager attached a one-page sheet called 'How to reduce visitor–patient infection'. There was nothing new in what she wrote, but it did address a concern that she was aware the hospital had and was written in a straightforward, sensible way.

An IT helpdesk staffer, going for promotion to manager, devised a set of suggestions for increasing the self-reliance and IT knowledge of the typical computer user, illustrated with snappy little cartoons from an artistically gifted brother. He called it 'Improving helpdesk happiness'.

## *Offering a case study*

Depending on your profession and the kind of job for which you are competing, you might also consider writing up a case study. The aim here would be to demonstrate your skills, commitment and knowledge. This can be a powerful aid to getting a job largely because the human element makes it interesting to read and shows how you work, as well as the results you typically get. If you do submit a case study, keep to a two-page limit and make sure you have comprehensively disguised the identity of the subject – or have their full permission to use it with any amendments they suggest to protect their reputation. Write in the first person. Here the format could be:

1 An introduction to the case: the people involved, brief character sketches.

2 What the challenges were and how they presented; what was at stake for you and for the people or organization involved.

3 What you did to overcome the challenges: what you tried; what worked well, what worked less well.

4 Lessons learnt – by you and the people involved.

5 Conclusions and general principles that could be applied elsewhere.

Some examples from my own clients have included accounts of:

how a company improved its enquiry and sales conversion rates from direct mail;

a training project which played an important part in improving customer satisfaction rates;

how one new drug successfully found its way through a regulator's tough requirements;

applying the principles of mediation in a libel case and why they worked.

All the methods I describe in this chapter can be compelling ways to increase respect for you as a candidate because they go beyond what the majority of your rivals will offer. But be cautious. The critical question is: How might this piece of communication be received? If the answer is with interest and approval, then go ahead.

# HIGH-IMPACT COVERING LETTERS

The covering letter is yet another way to stake your claim to the job, but there is an art in writing it well. This chapter explains how to construct a covering letter that will catch the employer's eye and boost your application.

You might assume that the covering letter is pointless – after all, you've written a magnificent CV, so why spend time composing another document? Perhaps this is why so many people make little effort at this point, writing something like this:

A. N. Applicant
Address
Postcode
E-mail

Mr A. B. Xxxxx
Head of Department
Employer Ltd
Postcode

Date

Dear Mr Xxxxx

I hereby enclose my CV to apply for the job of Y as advertised in *The Newspaper Chronicle*, < date >.

I look forward to hearing from you.

Yours sincerely

Ms A. N. Applicant

## The role of the covering letter

Writing a covering letter like this means you miss a further opportunity to impress the potential employer. Preparing to write this chapter, I conducted a mini telephone poll of a dozen friendly HR specialists. My question was: How much importance do you give to the covering letter? Nine of the 12 said they gave it considerable attention, using it as the first part of the screening process, and only two said they regarded it as unimportant. Three admitted that if the covering letter was poor, it meant that they did not bother to read the actual CV with any real attention. While this may seem shocking, it is the reality. When there is severe competition for jobs and any advertisement brings in dozens or even hundreds of applications, initial screening is bound to be cursory.

Three of my respondents also told me that where senior jobs were concerned, they preferred a covering letter to a CV, seeing it as an essential introductory step and, in fact, one of these HR people now routinely asks not for a CV but for a letter: what she called 'an expression of interest'. Only if the writer passes this initial scrutiny will she consider it worth her while to ask for a CV. So the traditional covering letter lives on and flourishes.

The covering letter can give a better flavour of your personality: it should convey the essence of your personal brand (Chapter 4). When it is elegantly set out, immaculately written and carefully composed to emphasize your skills, it gives you a chance to stand out from other candidates who have not taken so much trouble. It can draw attention to the headline version of how well you match what the employer has said they are looking for and can also give you a way to demonstrate your communication skills. One problem with CVs is that unless the employer has specifically asked you to say why you want the job, this element may not be obvious from your CV, whereas it is simple to state in a letter. It's also easy to miss one of the critical differences between a CV and a covering letter. The CV is an account of your past; it has a backward-looking purpose. The covering letter should focus on the future and point out what you can bring to the hiring organization. This is why the letter should never just be a straight repeat of everything on your CV.

The covering letter allows you to explain any obvious gaps in your work record, though you should weigh up whether or not you want to take the risk of drawing attention to such gaps in the first place (see Chapter 13 for advice on this).

There are two types of covering letter: the most usual is the letter that accompanies your CV for a job that has been advertised. The second type is a speculative letter where there is no known vacancy. These letters can be part of a general approach to job searching and their purpose is to set up an introductory meeting (see page 19), but many of the same principles apply to both.

## Ten top tips on getting covering letters right

1   Make it obviously different from your CV. The style, purpose and content of the letter should complement but not repeat the language and content of the CV. The letter should be more informal in style and tone, though not jokey or ingratiating, more like the kind of letter you might write to a professional acquaintance whom you respect but do not know well.

2   Take care with the salutation and sign-off. Never, ever, address your letter to Dear Sir or Madam or To Whom It May Concern. Remember how annoying it feels to get letters addressed to

Dear Resident, or Dear Colleague? These are the sure signs of junk mail and they go straight into the bin. Normally there will be a named person in the advertisement, often an HR professional, and this is the person you should address by name. If the named contact person is clearly a headhunter or HR professional, never try bypassing them and addressing the person you assume would be your boss if you got the job. All this will do is annoy everyone concerned. The boss is paying that contact person to spare them the trouble of dealing with the application process themself.

3   Beware of being too matey: never say Dear Chris to someone you have never met or spoken to. If you are unsure whether Chris is male or female, then this is easy to check out with the company's switchboard or through Facebook or LinkedIn. Where there is the slightest risk of seeming overfamiliar, then more formal is safer than less formal, so Dear Mr Jones is reliably respectful. When you are addressing a letter to a woman, check how she normally refers to herself. Personally, I respond well to someone who addresses me as Mrs Rogers, having taken the trouble to research that this is my married name, though Ms Rogers is also fine by me. I also find it perfectly OK where people use both names: Dear Chris Jones is increasingly acceptable as a compromise between the formality of Dear Ms Jones and the informality of Dear Chris. Where you have already had some correspondence with the employer, then follow their custom; so if they have addressed you as Dear Ms or Mr, you should do the same.

4   Get the address and name details correct. Be ultra-careful. It is amazing how many people make mistakes here – for instance, misspelling the name or putting a dash or apostrophe in the wrong place. If you are addressing the actual hiring manager, then look carefully at the details you have been sent about them, or check them out on the internet. Double-check where there are innumerable ways of spelling the same name – for instance Catherine, Catharine, Katherine, Kathryn, Katheryn, Katrin, Katarina, Catriona, Katrina, Katharine, Kathy, Kathie, Katie, Kati, Kath, Kat, Cathie, Cathy – or even Caitlin. Anyone with this kind of name will be super-sensitive to the many possibilities for getting it wrong and if you do, it will look as if you can't be bothered to be accurate. In some professions, it is customary to add qualifications and honours in every written communication.

So Professor Chris Jones, a distinguished doctor, may always add his Royal College affiliation and his other qualifications and if he has an honour, he may also add that. Although people always address him verbally as Chris, he may refer to himself in writing as Christopher. So when you put the addressee's name and address on your letter you should include all the qualifications and honours exactly as they appear on the job pack, eg Professor Christopher Jones CBE; MB, BCh, FRCOG.

It makes a typed letter much more personal when the salutation and sign-off are handwritten. When you sign off, it is unusual now to end the letter Yours truly. Yours sincerely is better. Avoid anything overfamiliar such as Yours ever, All the best or Cheers! Leave four spaces and type your name in caps beneath a handwritten signature. This helps the hiring organization get the spelling of your own name right. If you are in the habit of penning an undecipherable signature, take extra care in how you write your name. A massive flourish, nasty scrawl or huge heavily ornate calligraphy may undermine the impression you have been so careful to create in other ways. And definitely no green, purple or red ink. Black or blue are the only acceptable colours.

5 Keep it to one page. Where a covering letter goes on for longer than one page, the reader will lose interest. Just as a long CV suggests someone self-important and unable to edit their career to the essentials needed for the possible new job, an overlong covering letter will convey the same message. One A4 page comprising three or four well-spaced paragraphs is plenty.

6 Use lively, straightforward, direct language, avoiding all jargon and long-winded sentences.

7 Take care with presentation. Check and then double-check for typos and grammatical errors. As with the CV, use good-quality unlined white or pale cream A4 paper, never less than 100 gsm – and never that old-fashioned blue 'writing paper' or anything with flowers and sweet little pictures on it. The envelope should be a matching good-quality paper in A4 to minimize folding, and stout enough to reduce the chances of damage in transit. Unless the employer has specifically asked you to restrict your application to e-mail, always send a letter and CV by post, whether as back-up to an electronic application or as the main document. Addressing the envelope

by hand and marking it Personal and Confidential makes it more likely to be opened by the addressee and clear that it is not junk mail. Check the cost of postage if you are using a large envelope: you do not want to annoy the employer by making them pay a surcharge. An e-mail is easy to miss or delete by accident; an actual letter written and delivered on paper is relatively unusual now. This makes it far more likely that it will be opened and read by the recipient.

**8**   Be positive. Always bear in mind the employer's question: Why should I be interested in you? The covering letter is not the place for over-modesty; it is the place to stake your claim to the job by showing the employer what benefits you would bring to them.

**9**   Tailor the letter. Just as there should be no such thing as a standard CV, there can be no such thing as a standard covering letter. A persuasive letter might well take you the best part of half a day to compose, but this will be time well spent. The tone of the letter should reflect the job and the sector, so drama and whizziness might be exactly right for a job in an ad agency whereas something more austere would be better if you are looking for work with the civil service. Check this out as part of your research into the job.

**10**  End with a clear message. This might include stating when you are available for interview – for instance, you may have a long-booked holiday coming up in the next few weeks – if so, you should say so. Wherever possible you should state that you will be the one to make the next move. The initiative lies with you and not with the employer. So you might end with the hope that you will be interviewed and that you will call to find out if you have made the shortlist, or, if it is a speculative letter, that you will call to set up a meeting or phone call.

# A useful framework

## At the top

Set out all your home contact details – see page 160 for more detail on this. Take care with the letterhead. This should be consistent with the CV: the same typeface and general layout.

Addressee's name and address set out two spaces down and left aligned, single spaced.

Date set out two spaces below the addressee's details.

The salutation: using the stated contact person's name (see above).

Put all the reference details of the job, its actual name and any reference number, plus the place and date where you saw the advertisement, between the salutation and the first paragraph of the letter. The employer may be recruiting for several posts at once and you want to make it as easy as possible for them to identify you.

## First paragraph

**Things never to do or say**. You potentially waste an opportunity if you merely do what 99 per cent of job applicants do – which is to write what is already obvious: that you are applying for a job and enclosing or attaching your CV. Learn from newspaper reporters and novelists, both of whom, if they have any sense, make the first paragraph the one that ensures the reader keeps on reading. Here are some actual quotes from covering letters which ensured that the person scuppered their chances immediately:

| Opening statement | Impression |
|---|---|
| I was made redundant a year ago and I still haven't found a job. | Must be something wrong with you, then. |
| I can do anything and have no special preferences for a role. | No one wants this kind of alleged generalist. |
| Please, please give me a chance, I am desperate. | Desperation does not sell. |
| Research proves that a successful company needs dedicated R&D staff who can get the product pipeline going. | Yes, we know, that's why we're in the process of hiring one. |
| I am a competent strategic transformation specialist with a functionalist background in mechanical engineering fully appraised of the requirements of the modern marketing paradigm. | Mmm, but maybe not a clear communicator? |

Tactics that work:

> Mention the name of someone the hiring manager respects or knows:
>
>> Tracy Blackwood, a colleague of mine in the Customer Relations Society, has strongly encouraged me to apply for this role.
>
> Express informed admiration of the company:
>
>> I have watched the growth of AB Holdings with admiration, waiting for the right chance to apply for a job with you. I believe my skills are an excellent match to what you need for the job of < job title >.
>
> Lead in with a mention of a high-profile employer or educational course:
>
>> As someone who has just completed the Cabinet Office leadership course, I believe I am ready for ...
>
>> After five years at Marks & Spencer headquarters in a senior post, I would welcome the chance of bringing my skills to the job of < job title >.
>
> State the length of time you have been interested in the role and/or career:
>
>> My interest in fashion retailing started at age 6 when I became a discerning buyer of pocket-money accessories for little girls and it has continued ever since, though now my taste has developed to the high-fashion end of the business.
>
>> Ever since I can remember, I have been interested in teaching: fascinated by watching my own teachers and an eager learner myself.
>
> Identify yourself immediately in your professional role:
>
>> As a versatile and experienced PA to the chief executive in my current role, I am intrigued and excited by the possibility of working as senior PA to your chief executive.
>
> Go straight for enthusiasm:
>
>> Your job immediately appealed to me when I saw it advertised because < one-sentence summary >.

Go for cheeky and confident (with caution, and only in sectors where this behaviour is valued):

My application will show you that I stand out from my peers. Where they went to university at 18, I started work as a runner for TVWorld Productions. Where they spent time studying media theory, I got immediately involved in media practice. Where they struggled to find any work at 21, I was already directing my own films.

## Second paragraph

The second paragraph describes what attracts you to the company and the job – in that order. All employers want to believe that the world is vying to work for them. If you are not enthusiastic about the potential employer, then probably you should not be applying for the job. This paragraph is the place to give a warm summary of your research into the company and the vacant post. Elements you may want to consider including could be:

- Why you endorse the company's or unit's mission and purpose. Normally this will be because it is a good match to your own values and deeply held beliefs. Look at the company's website to see what they say about themselves.

- Any personal experience you have of its products and services and how this has increased your motivation.

- Briefly mentioning the challenges that your research into the job has revealed – or that the job pack states and why it would attract you to tackle them.

- Naming what motivates most people who have this job and saying why you share it.

Examples:

Sian is a musician and is looking for freelance work teaching piano and singing to small children. She is applying to an independent company which acts as broker/agent for schools:

I have been greatly impressed by the professionalism I have seen in The Music Factory. Two of your associates taught in the school where I was also working freelance last year (Bigfield Primary) and their work and dedication spoke volumes for the high standards on which you clearly insist. Your website sings out with the love of music and the importance it must and should have in young children's lives – something I share. I get enormous satisfaction from teaching music, especially piano to very small children who are too young to consider it 'difficult'. It would be a privilege to join your associate team to do this work.

William is a law graduate working as a paralegal in a large City law firm and is applying to join a trainee solicitor scheme:

Ever since my undergraduate days at Bristol University I have been aware of your firm and have admired the rapid way you have grown from only two principals to 14. Your niche, human rights and equality, is intensely competitive yet you have established a sector-wide reputation for superb work, often with cases that other law firms will not take on. This cause is close to my own heart: I worked as a volunteer for Amnesty International during two vacations, worked as office assistant for XY firm of solicitors, specialists in immigration appeals, during another vacation and in my current paralegal work have played a leading role supporting our solicitors and counsel in the case of X v Y: < a high-profile case involving human rights >.

## Third paragraph: a summary of your skills and experience

Your CV will set this out in detail but the covering letter needs to give a convincing summary. Your task here is to unpick what the employer says they want and to show what a good match you are. Choose from the following ways of doing it.

## A narrative summary

Example: Tim is looking for work as a retail sales manager. The employer has said they want the following: five years of sales experience in a retail environment; skill in handling complaints; experience of managing junior staff; inventory control; evidence of increases in sales. Tim makes sure that his letter reflects these criteria exactly:

At Frantic Records in Oxford St, London I was promoted a year ago to assistant manager after 4 years in the Knightsbridge branch as senior sales assistant. This is a fast-paced retail environment needing skilled management of staff and customers. I took over daily responsibility for managing customer complaints with the aim of ensuring that customers returned and had a positive experience of shopping with us. I took special responsibility for training our largely young and inexperienced Saturday/Sunday staff. Stock control is an important part of my job. I am proud of the fact that sales have increased by 15% over the last year and feel I have made an important contribution here.

Example: Frances is a young social worker with three years' experience and a strong interest in child protection. She wants promotion but there are no opportunities in her current local authority because there have been budget cuts. Reflecting precisely the requirements set out in the job ad, she writes:

As a summary of how my skills and experience match what you seek, I am a graduate (University of Sheffield, History Honours, 2.1) and a GSCC-qualified social worker, current CRB, with 3 years' front-line experience in a busy child protection team at XY Council. I am 100% committed to the importance of child protection and am thoroughly familiar with the legislative framework in which we operate. I enjoy teamwork and understand how vital it is to act flexibly with colleagues in this demanding work. My assessment and analytical skills are first rate. I pride myself on my ability to communicate well with vulnerable children and their parents and manage a demanding case load currently, which includes completing S47 investigations, care assessments and instigating care proceedings.

## A bullet point list or table

Example: Tina is applying for a job as an audit specialist in a midwifery unit. Again, she has gutted the rather long-winded job description for the essential experience and qualities that the job seems to require and writes:

I believe I am an excellent match to the experience and skills you need:

| You need | I offer |
| --- | --- |
| A registered midwife with 3+ years of post-registration experience | 6 years of post-registration experience in the Maternity Unit at Blanstone District General Hospital. |
| Experience of managing records | At Blanstone I have managed the Care Records Service on the post-natal ward, ensuring that senior managers had timely and accurate information on patients and clinical results. |
| Managing staff | As the Senior Midwife I have had responsibility for recruiting, training and managing staff including a special project for newly qualified midwives; liaised with Community Nursing Services to improve our home births system. |
| IT/project-management skills | Hold Prince 2 Foundation and Practitioner certificates; confident in using Word, Excel and PowerPoint. Ran the New Mother and Baby Project for the trust, achieving 3-star award. |
| Advocate for women | I became a midwife because I believe in the importance of protecting and promoting the needs of pregnant women and new mothers. Advocacy has been an important part of my work at Blanstone. |

Example: Jean-Paul trained as a vet but never practised and went into a sales role instead. He is applying for a job as territory manager for Southern Europe in a pharmaceutical company. The company sells veterinary products. The job description and person specification are skimpy but he homes in on the few elements they have stated by giving a crisp bullet point list set out as a table:

This is a brief overview of how I match what you are looking for:

| | |
|---|---|
| Veterinary qualification (UCL, 2005) | Bilingual French and English, fluent in Spanish; some knowledge of Portuguese |
| Keen interest in animal health and welfare | Lived for 10 years in Toulouse and know both French and Spanish cultures well |
| 4 years' experience as senior sales representative for AMB Veterinary Products plc | Managerial experience: currently run sales team of 5 |
| Increased sales year on year by 10% | Fully eligible to live and work in UK/EU |

## Emphasize the problems you can solve for the employer

Jobs exist because employers have problems that they cannot solve in other ways. If a job or the person doing it is no longer adding value through solving problems, either the job or the person doing it is eliminated. It is essential to spend time researching what these problems might be (Chapter 5), so that you will know how to suggest that you could solve them. Be careful of assuming that on the basis of a little research you will know everything about the company, because you will not. Also, you need to be tactful in how you phrase your suggestions. 'Your company is failing and I can save it' is unlikely to be received with a jolly smile, especially where the person who receives your letter is the one largely responsible for such failure.

Example: Ethan is a recently graduated Politics PhD committed to an academic career. He knows that in many universities the senior staff are more interested in research and publishing than in teaching and often regard teaching as a chore. He enjoys teaching, is good at it and does not much enjoy research. However, undergraduates are more interested in teaching than in research. There is increasing pressure from dissatisfied students and their parents, now paying hard cash for education, to improve the quantity and quality of teaching as well as making other opportunities to connect with students. In applying for a teaching assistant role at XY University, Ethan writes:

> I have discovered a love of teaching and positively seek opportunities to lead seminars, facilitate discussions and introduce key ideas in 21st-century Politics to undergraduates.
> Last year I completed and self-funded the Westminster Pastoral Foundation course in Counselling and this has deepened my skill as well as my willingness to offer support and counselling to individual students.

## Final paragraph

You can use the final paragraph in a number of ways:

As a straight sign-off:

> All my contact details are above and I hope to hear that you have put me on your shortlist.

Stating your availability for interview. Employers are not very rational here. It is part of the employer mindset to believe that applicants should be willing to change any personal arrangement in order to make themselves available. If you really are unwilling to sacrifice your holiday because it is so expensive or so vital to your health and wellbeing, then accept that you may miss your chance. Where your application is a strong one, a sensible employer may be willing to rearrange the selection process to accommodate you, but my experience is that this is rare:

> I have a holiday booked in the US from May 21 to 28 so would not be able to attend an interview during that time but can be flexible before and after that.

> My final exams take place in the week of May 5–12 but I am free after that and hope to hear that you will be calling me to an interview.

> I am getting married on March 31 with a honeymoon planned for the following week, but will be available for interview from April 10.

> With a little notice I can travel to London at any time and look forward to hearing from you.

As a way of underlining your interest in the role:

> Finally, I emphasize my enthusiasm for this role and look forward to discussing it with you in person.

> This job encapsulates everything that enthuses me about my work. I believe I am an excellent match to your needs and hope to meet you to explore how we can take this further.

> This letter and my CV probably cannot adequately convey my drive, resourcefulness, sense of personal mission and commitment. I admire what XY Ltd does and would be a fully committed team member. I hope to be able to demonstrate this at interview and look forward to hearing from you.

Saying that you will call to find out what the status of your application is, though note that some employers specifically discourage this where you are replying to a job ad and the employer expects a large response because it is a mass recruitment exercise – for instance, for graduate entry-level posts.

Never underestimate the importance of the covering letter: it gives you a valuable additional chance to stake your claim to the job.

# 12

# THE FINE ART OF PRESENTATION

We live in an age where outstanding graphic design is taken for granted, and this chapter explores how to ensure that your CV looks good and reads well. It cannot afford to look amateurish or miserably old-fashioned. You may feel that when so many job applications are submitted electronically, this does not matter, but actually it does. The more senior the job, the more likely it is that you will be asked to send a CV as an e-mail attachment; this will be printed off as hard copy for the shortlisters and eventually for the selection panel. I also advise you to send a hard copy by post as a back-up, something that many employers ask for anyway. A well-designed CV shows selectors that you are self-confident, stylish and have a contemporary outlook, qualities that all employers value, whereas a poor piece of graphic design suggests someone slapdash, out of date or not self-aware.

## Mistakes to avoid

There are a number of common mistakes that I see in the early drafts of CVs:

- People who understand that two pages are the limit, but feel they can get around this by fiddling the margins or reducing the type size. Don't do this: as a ruse it fails miserably because it is so obvious.

- Clumsy use of white space, typically using single spacing everywhere with two presses of the Enter key to create more space.

- Fancy fonts, for instance faux-handwriting fonts such as Lucida Handwriting. These are difficult to read and are unsuitable for a professional communication, so avoid them. The impact can be that the writer seems girlish and simpering – not a good impression.

- A riot of fonts. The writer wants to express their inner graphic designer and goes mad, mixing three or four different fonts and sizes.

- Inconsistent spacing and headings; variations in indenting and bullet points. This looks messy and amateurish.

- Inexperienced typist mistakes: accepting the default font and type size offered by the computer. Omitting spaces between sentences.

## How to create a visually attractive CV

*Lay out your contact details stylishly.* Opinions are divided about whether it is better to put them to the left, right or centre of the document. The case for left justify is that the human eye tends to fall on this side of the page first. The case for right justify is that an HR professional riffling through a large number of applications will see a right-justified heading first. Centring gives you some visual contrast. There's no one right way: it's up to you.

Save space by keeping your address to the minimum number of lines; for instance, you don't need a county or district name. Do use a new line for the postcode, however. Use single spacing for the actual address. It's not necessary to write 'Curriculum vitae' at the top of the document: it will be obvious that this is what the document is.

People sometimes confuse a CV with something official such as a passport application. Remember that the CV is a marketing document, and should not be confused with getting security clearance or applying for a grant. Just put your name at the top and unless you are known by all your names, there is no need to include your middle name or names. The employer is not interested in the fact that your parents tried to flatter their parents by giving you your grandmothers' maiden names as part of yours. Two names are enough unless you are actually double-barrelled. If you are generally known by a shortened or anglicized version of your name, then use that on your CV. So Michael Jones has been known as Mike for the last 20 years and he refers to himself this way on his CV. Jiang Li was born in Hong Kong but has lived in the UK for 25 years and now calls herself Joanne Lee, so this is what appears on her CV.

Include all your contact details: home address, home e-mail, Skype address, landline and mobile numbers. Don't make the mistake of having a jumbo-sized font for your name and then 11 or 12 point for the body of the document: it looks egotistical. Adding bold or italic to the normal font is usually enough to give a little emphasis if this is what you want. Have a professional-sounding e-mail address, ideally one that is short, easily spelt and easily remembered. This should be consistent with the impression you want to give. So if you share a jokey e-mail address with your partner, now might be the time to consider changing to something that sounds more grown up and serious. Johnjosieanddogs@crazy.net might amuse your friends but it is unlikely to impress an employer.

Don't include your current business contact details (address, e-mail and phone number) unless you are freelance, as this will give the impression that you are using your workplace for job-search purposes. Also, it could annoy your current employer if they get evidence that this is indeed what you are doing.

It can look attractive to add a single line or shaded bar under your contact details to separate it visually from what follows. Stick to the same font that you have chosen for the rest of the document.

*Use white space effectively.* Keep to standard margins, however tempting it may seem to reduce them. The default for Word is either 3.17 cm at each side and 2.54 cm top and bottom, or 2.54 cm on each side as well as top and bottom, depending on which version of Word you use. These have been chosen because they look good, so don't play with them: your page will look cramped if you do. Many people don't know that there is a middle option between the lack of space created by single spacing and getting too much by pressing the Enter key twice. In Word, highlight the areas you want to be affected, go to the Format menu or Home; click on the Paragraph drop-down menu. In the Spacing box, choose Before and set to 6 pt. This creates more than a single space and less than a double. Alternatively, select the text and choose the line-spacing option, either 1.15 or 1.5 and see what effect that has on the way the document looks.

*Fonts.* Classic fonts are always safe. One tip is to copy the font that the employer has used in their job pack: a subtle piece of matching. Failing that, stick to fonts that are easy to read and have no over-elaborate curly bits or funny thick bits. Helvetica, Trebuchet, Gill Sans MT, Times New Roman and Arial are all good choices. There is some evidence that fonts such as Times New Roman with serifs (the little tips at the ends of letters) are easier to read than sans-serif typefaces such as Arial, but this probably does not matter too much in a short document. Never choose the condensed or narrow versions of these fonts, again often resorted to by people desperate to add more words within the allowed two pages of a CV. It is self-defeating because you immediately make the text harder to read. Stick to 11 or 12 point. Anything smaller is too small and anything larger looks grandiose and crude. Where you are tempted to reduce the font size it is always because you have too many words, so the cure is to reduce the words, not the type size. The right number of words for a CV is about 500.

Your covering letter (Chapter 11) should be in the same style: identical fonts and contact details. This will convey consistency, thoughtfulness and organization to the person who reads them.

*Colour and graphics.* Stick to black. People sometimes produce subtly printed grey or pale navy CVs, not realizing that the original is frequently copied and that with each copy the type becomes fainter. Rainbow printing and shaded second-colour headings may work on the internet or in a book but they are out of place in a CV, not least because the employer will probably copy them in monochrome anyway. Software now makes it easy to include fancy graphics, for instance clip art, company logos and so on. Avoid adding anything like this. Unless you are a professional graphic designer it will look naive and unprofessional. Also, if you are e-mailing the CV, the recipient's browser may not be able to cope with whatever graphics you have added.

*Justification.* Keep to left justify. If you have left and right justification it is harder to read and will also produce strange blank spaces in the text.

*Bullets.* Choose straightforward bullets: simple dots or squares. Avoid ticks, fancy splodges or smiley faces. It is possible to overdo bullet points, so use them sparingly as too many on one page looks fussy. Eight is a good rule of thumb as the maximum per page.

*Headings.* These should be in the same typeface as the rest of the text. Use bold or bold italic. Don't underline: it looks old-fashioned and is unnecessary when bold does the same job.

*Page breaks.* Watch out for clumsy page breaks – for instance, letting the last line of a section drift over to the next page or having a heading that is the bottom line of one page and is thus separated from the text it introduces. It is normally relatively easy to tighten or loosen the text to ensure that this cannot happen. These design irritations are known as 'widows and orphans' in the printing trade. You cannot always control how an e-mailed document will appear on the recipient's computer. I once received a draft CV from a client whose own computer confined it to two pages, but, mysteriously, it spread to five on mine. However, you can certainly ensure that it looks neat when you print it out and send it by post.

*Footers.* People often forget to add page numbers. This is important because the document will be printed out if you have e-mailed it and copied if you have sent it by post, so the pages may get separated. For the same reason, type < your name > CV page 1 as your footer and give the job reference number and name. Use 9-point italic as this is small enough to be discreet but easily spotted if necessary.

*Stapled or not?* Secure the pages with a paper clip when you send the CV by post. The employer will want to copy your CV and if it is stapled it is annoying to have to remove the staple.

*Printing.* A laser printer gives a sharper, cleaner result than inkjet. Dot matrix printers belong in the Science Museum. If you have a cheap inkjet printer, then copy your CV and letter on to a memory stick and take it to a friend or colleague who has a better-quality machine. Never photocopy a CV as you will reduce the clarity of the print.

*Paper.* For a CV that you are going to hand personally to others or send by post, this is not the time to economize on paper. Paper is cheap anyway, but you should choose good-quality plain white or very light cream A4 size, ideally the type of paper that is called 'laid', meaning that it has a slightly ribbed texture that is pleasant to handle. But try out the paper with the printer first as with some laid paper you may get a slightly smudged effect, especially with inkjet printers. If you choose ordinary paper, make sure its weight is 100 gsm or more – the weight is clearly marked on the pack. Heavier, better-quality paper immediately suggests a person of substance and will also be far more resistant to damage in handling, whether in transit or during the selection process. Use an A4 envelope so that you do not have to fold the document and buy an envelope that is good quality as it is a pity to spoil the good impression created by high-quality paper in the CV itself if the envelope in which it arrives is an obvious buy from the bargain bin at your local stationery shop.

# The difference that layout can make

The client I will call James Balham asked me for help with his CV and brought me the first part of it to review:

---

*CURRICULUM VITAE*

## JAMES MORGAN BALHAM

56 Market House

150 St Germain St

Pelham

Nottinghamshire

NT 16 0BD

JB234@googlemail.com

Mobile: 07777 775634

---

**Objective**: management trainer with 7 years' outstanding experience of working in local authorities, improving results and participant satisfaction, looking for a job as training manager in a public sector organization

---

**Experience and Skill**

**Senior training consultant, Passmore Council, <date to date>**

- ❖ High level skills in facilitation: have run groups of all sorts successfully and can deal with any crisis that occurs
- ❖ Excellent presentation skills: consistently get feedback that explanations are clear, compelling and entertaining. Can deliver without notes or PowerPoint
- ❖ Fully up to date on modern management theories and ideas. Have delivered courses on subjects as varied as Business Process Re-engineering, Servant Leadership, Effective Teamworking, Managing Performance and Handling Difficult Staff
- ❖ Successfully competed for a bursary place at high level course at Columbia University, NY, Group Dynamics: A Systems Perspective (ORL 5362) 2010. This course deepened my understanding of the theoretical aspects of facilitation

❖ Developed new and effective methodology for collecting and analysing feedback from participants on courses allowing us to make substantial improvements in the quality of our offer, eliminating unsuccessful course and promoting the successful ones

❖ Increased overall satisfaction score on Department's courses from 60% to 89%. This resulted in increased funding for the department as well as raising its profile in the Authority generally. 35% of the Authority's managerial staff have attended at least one of our events in the past year: an increase of 40% on the rate three years ago.

❖ Handled annual budgets of £500,000; reduced deficit from 20% to zero over 3 years

❖ Introduced tailored courses to Department's portfolio, working as consultant to Authority's senior managers, developing specially designed courses on subjects as varied as Coaching for Change, Managing Change and Finance for Non-financial Managers. Increased number of such courses by 35% in last financial year

The content is fine as it stands, in fact it is persuasive, but if James had carried on with this CV it would easily have stretched to four or even five pages. James has used an enormous typeface, Bodoni, for his name, and has said the document is a CV when it is already obvious that it is a CV. He has spread out his address details with double spacing, added boxes which give a fussy impression and has used Verdana, a different typeface, for the rest of the document. There is no footer. The fancy bullets are a distraction when so much else is going on visually. Although Verdana is an easy typeface to read on screen it is extremely sprawly and takes up an enormous amount of space, even when used with single spacing. In fact, the single spacing also makes it difficult to read. No wonder James was worried about how he was going to follow my rule of 'no more than two pages' as he had yet to describe his earlier career or qualifications.

In the revised version, the content is exactly the same but by reformatting the document, it fits easily on one page and is much easier to read:

JAMES BALHAM
*56 Market House, 150 St Germain St*
*Pelham*
*NT 16 0BD*[1][2]
JB234@googlemail.com
Mobile: 07777 775634

---

*Objective*: management trainer with 7 years' outstanding experience of working in local authorities, improving results and participant satisfaction, looking for a job as training manager in a public sector organization[3]

---

### Experience and skills

#### Senior training consultant, Passmore Council, < date >to< date >

- High-level skills in facilitation: have run groups of all sorts successfully and can deal with any crisis that occurs.[4]

- Excellent presentation skills: consistently get feedback that explanations are clear, compelling and entertaining. Can deliver without notes or PowerPoint.

- Fully up to date on modern management theories and ideas. Have delivered courses on subjects as varied as Business Process Re-engineering, Servant Leadership, Effective Teamworking, Managing Performance and Handling Difficult Staff.

- Successfully competed for a bursary place at high-level course at Columbia University, NY, Group Dynamics: A Systems Perspective (ORL 5362) 2010. This course deepened my understanding of the theoretical aspects of facilitation.

- Developed new and effective methodology for collecting and analysing feedback from participants on courses, allowing us to make substantial improvements in the quality of our offer, eliminating unsuccessful course and promoting the successful ones.

- Increased overall satisfaction score on department's courses from 60% to 89%. This resulted in increased funding for the department as well as raising its profile in the Authority generally. 35% of the Authority's managerial staff have attended at least one of our events in the past year: an increase of 40% on the rate three years ago.

- Handled annual budgets of £500,000; reduced deficit from 20% to zero over 3 years.

- Introduced tailored courses to department's portfolio, working as consultant to Authority's senior managers, developing specially designed courses on subjects as varied as Coaching for Change, Managing Change and Finance for Non-financial Managers. Increased number of such courses by 35% in last financial year.[5]

[1]　Address reduced to 3 lines.

[2]　Same typeface and size as rest of document but in bold italic. Gill Sans Std typeface looks contemporary; font size is relatively small, although this is 12 pt and therefore still highly readable.

[3]　A box surrounding his career objective is now fine as it is not competing with a box above it.

[4]　Better spacing between bullets introduces welcome white space. Slightly fancy bullets now acceptable when rest of document has been simplified.

[5]　Footer added.

## Sending CVs by e-mail

When you send a CV as an attachment to an e-mail it is better to stick to straightforward fonts and to minimize design features. The recipient's computer may have different software, turning your carefully formatted document into something that looks distinctly weird – for instance, it may insert extra pages or turn a bulleted list into plain text. There are exceptions here – for instance, if you are applying for a job where visual design is important then it will be essential to produce a CV which demonstrates your capabilities, but check in this case whether it will be acceptable before you send it. Usually you are safe with standard fonts, normal margins and simple text enhancements such as italic or bold. Never send a CV as a zip file – zipping is for over-large documents and it looks pretentious to apply it to a short document like a CV. Don't attach as an .exe file as this may be rejected by the recipient's firewall on the understandable grounds that so many of them contain viruses. It is not safe to put your contact details as a header or footer because if the recipient copies the CV using the Select All option, the software may miss out the headers and footers. Inserted text boxes may suffer the same fate. The employer may specify some of this in their instructions, but if you are applying on spec, you may not know.

Save the CV with your name and whichever CV version it is plus some reference to the job, for instance KHolmes CV CallCentre TeamLeader. This will make it easy for you to identify for later reference and will also make it easy for the employer to do the same.

If in doubt there are two other tactics you can consider:

- Remove all the extra features and save the CV as a plain text document, which will now have *.txt in its title. The disadvantage is that this makes for a much duller look but it is certainly safe and will be accepted by any software at the receiving end.

- Save your CV in PDF format, in other words as a read-only document. This will preserve all its features and is also a simple first-level defence against another person tampering with it.

# EMBARRASSMENTS AND HOW TO HANDLE THEM

There are few careers without at least a little associated embarrassment. This chapter deals with examples, whether they are something mild like having stayed in one organization for longer than now seems wise, or a major disadvantage like a criminal conviction.

When my clients discuss this topic with me, they often speak yearningly of 'career plans', implying that somewhere out there are people who devised a career strategy when they were young and then have made it all happen like clockwork. I have never met such a person. Instead I observe that the grand patterns of our careers are largely governed by external forces such as trends in society, access to higher education and the effects of international competition on the leading sectors in our regions. Not least, the overall state of the economy at any one time can bring jobs to an abrupt halt and it is no longer unusual for an individual to have experienced redundancy several times. The dominant pattern in the middle of the 20th century was of long-lasting careers in one organization or sector, but international competition and rapid changes in technology have meant that such careers are now the exception rather than the rule. All of this can create difficulties when you are presenting your CV but you do need to put your own experience into a wider context before you panic. Most employers will understand this bigger picture and at least some of them will be generous and measured about how they interpret any particular glitch in your own CV.

## Spinning, lies and fraud

Unfortunately, it seems that many candidates do not believe in the mercifulness and maturity of employers and bend the truth in writing a CV. 'Spinning' your CV to present the strongest possible case is one thing; lies and fraud are another altogether. A survey in 2005 by the Risk Advisory Group, a consultancy specializing in risk assessments of all sorts including employee screening, found that more than 50 per cent of the 3,700 CVs they surveyed contained some warping of the truth. Other surveys have claimed that at least 20 per cent of CVs contain misrepresentations. The most common lies concern distortions about previous jobs, for instance exaggerating seniority or reinventing the job title to sound more impressive, giving misleading information about dates of employment or academic qualifications and making up or exaggerating academic achievement. Undisclosed directorships, bankruptcies and county court judgements are common omissions – information that is often requested where the job involves handling money. Straight lies concern qualifications that have been bought from non-existent universities, forged or 'lost' qualifications and fraudulent references. Every now and again, the lies or deceptions are uncovered to expose someone in a senior job, who might perhaps be expected to know better than to risk their career:

- The NHS administrator who was jailed in 2010 for wrongly claiming that she had the A levels which were the minimum needed to apply for the job and had backed up her application with forged references.

- The allegedly distinguished author and researcher from whom the offer of a professorial chair at a prestigious US university was withdrawn when it was discovered that he did not have the PhD he claimed.

- The eye surgeon who forged references from colleagues and also failed to mention that he had been suspended from his

job after previously having been caught lying on his CV.
He was struck off the medical register.

- Nick Leeson, the employee who brought Barings Bank to its
knees, did not disclose the county court judgements against
him when he applied for a job, something that might well have
made the bank hesitate about employing him.

People in public life are clearly not immune from the temptation to lie
about their less than impressive qualifications and career histories.
David Edmundson, chief executive of Radio Shack, the third largest
electronics retailer in the USA, eventually admitted he had falsely
claimed to have BSc degrees and lost his job as a result. The TV pre-
senter and nutritionist 'Dr' Gillian McKeith acquired her 'doctorate' by
correspondence from a 'college' that is not recognized anywhere as
an accredited educational establishment and she is not medically
qualified. Patrick Imbardelli was about to be promoted to the board
of Intercontinental Hotels when a tip-off revealed that he had never
completed the three courses from which he claimed to have graduated. Alison Ryan was dismissed from her job as head of communications for Manchester United after it was discovered that she had been
debarred by the Bar Council for professional misconduct after upping
her Cambridge degree to a first. The celebrity chef Gordon Ramsay
claimed to have had a first division football career cut tragically short by
injury when it seems that he merely played in one testimonial game.

# Why it matters not to lie

The many high-profile cases of CV lying have been turned into good
business by the increasing numbers of specialist agencies who can
be hired to check every single claim on your CV. This is because it
seems that one lie leads to another and then another. When a CV
is revealed to be 'misleading', on average there are three such dis-
crepancies in it. The agency will call every awarding body to check
whether you have the qualifications you claim and will also contact
every employer on your CV to verify that you actually worked there in
the job you name and for the dates and at the salary you state. When
employers do not outsource this work, they are increasingly likely to
investigate your claims themselves.

Routine checks are now much more common all round. For instance,
many employers will not bother with actual references, but even the

most unsystematic may now contact the previous employers listed on your CV, asking them to confirm the exact dates you were in the job, your job title and salary. I was once approached by an employer who wanted to offer a job to a young woman who had worked briefly as my secretary. She was desperate to get into an editorial role in publishing and had described her job with me as editorial assistant – the same title as the job for which she was applying. She had also awarded herself a higher salary than she had actually earned and had extended her alleged period of employment by six months. If you inflate your salary, the new employer will probably also discover the discrepancy through the local Inland Revenue office.

When you claim qualifications and experience that you don't have, you run the risk of being exposed during the interview. Standards of interviewing can still be disgracefully low, but in general they have risen steeply over the last few years. Many employers have now had training in how to interview and will probe your claims to experience. If these are based on flimsy lies, you will not convince. OK, so the only penalty in this case is that you will not get the job – but do you really want to be humiliated in this way?

If you do somehow get through this process, and your appointment was based on a significant inflation of the qualifications and experience that are essential in order to do the job, the chances are that you will underperform when doing it. This has been the undoing of many of those who have falsified their CVs. One of my clients discovered that a senior facilities manager in her organization had claimed two first-class degrees which he turned out not to possess, plus experience that he had not had. Her suspicions were aroused when his performance in the most basic parts of his job soon fell puzzlingly below what she had had every reason to expect. He was dismissed for gross misconduct.

Some young graduates lie about their qualifications, for instance to get a job abroad, gambling on the unlikelihood of a foreign employer checking unfamiliar qualifications and hoping that the deception is merely a short-term expedient. They may find that they are indeed successful in the job and get promoted. It can then become impossible to abandon the lie because it has become part of the story that others tell about them as well as the story they have been telling about themselves. Once people get to the levels of seniority where even just local fame means they are written up in newspapers, the danger of being unmasked rises. I have occasionally encountered successful senior people who do confess such exaggerations and lies to me under seal of confidentiality as their coach, describing the hideous stress of the deception, the increasing amounts of negative energy needed to maintain it and the constant fear of exposure. It is also easy to see how an unfriendly contact from your past could spitefully reveal lies and distortions and sometimes do so for money if they think the press will be interested in the story.

Be truthful with everyone involved in the recruitment process, otherwise you could find yourself tangled up in your own falsehoods. One young woman of my acquaintance was about to be offered a banking job at a million-pound salary plus bonus. When she stubbornly refused to state her current salary to the potential employer it became clear that she had implied a much bigger sum to the headhunter than she was in fact earning. The job offer was withdrawn.

Be alert to the seriousness of the warning if the employer tells you that you will need security clearance or vetting: they will mean it. For instance, for some civil service or other government roles where sensitive information is involved, you can expect to fill in an unusually detailed application form asking for information about your parents, your political activities and your financial status. A young friend with an unimpeachably bland and conventional career gave me as one of his referees for such a post and I was interviewed at considerable length and with great skill by a person whose sole job was to sniff out security risks. I was asked searching questions about his religious beliefs and practices, his political views, his sexuality, any possible addictions or substance misuse, his friendships, the state of his marriage and finances, many of which I found I could not actually answer in any detail. But I was left in no doubt that were there anything untoward in his past or present (there wasn't), the process of interrogating his four referees would certainly have uncovered it.

In an internet-savvy world, Google is a swift way to see how people describe themselves. For instance, one client of mine, frantic to get on shortlists, believed that her age was what was telling against her. She had taken five years off her age but was exposed when the employer found her Facebook page – which gave her real date of birth.

If it turns out that you have lied, you could be laying yourself open to criminal prosecution for obtaining pecuniary advantage by deception. One such manager in the NHS was given a two-year suspended sentence after he had claimed to have a degree and diploma from Nottingham Trent University when in fact his most impressive qualification was two A levels. He had been offered the job at a six-figure salary in preference to a candidate who did have the required qualifications.

If you are discovered to have lied once you are actually in the job, you will most probably be instantly dismissed and the employer is unlikely to give you a reference, thus making it even tougher to find another job. This is because the employer will conclude, rightly or wrongly, that a willingness to lie on your CV may suggest someone who is untrustworthy in other parts of their lives. Even if there is no criminal prosecution, the employer could sue you for material misrepresentation, pursuing you for the costs involved in your appointment, your salary and replacement. Few employers will actually do this because most employees will not have enough assets to make it worthwhile, but many might be prepared to threaten you with such action as a form of punishment for the stress and difficulty you have caused. Even something apparently bland like distorting or softening the significance of a health problem may land you in trouble. One local authority boss was sued for more than a million pounds after being accused of covering up a history of treatment for depression when she had applied for the job. The council sued to obtain reimbursement of the generous ill-health retirement pension it had awarded her as well as its legal fees. There was a long history of fractious relationships behind this case and the action failed, but it is a sign of how far an employer might go if they feel misled. In fact, asking about health status at application stage is now against the law, but the general principle of honesty about your health still applies.

Some people justify their CV lies by claiming that in an increasingly tight jobs market it is the only way to get work. Others will jauntily assert that employers lie about jobs so why shouldn't jobseekers lie in return? This last is a peculiar claim indeed. I have never known an employer to lie about a job, or understood what possible reason they could have for doing so, though I have known many who are unhelpfully confused about what it is that they actually want or need. In any case, as the wise saying has it, two wrongs do not make a right. It is dishonest to lie on your CV, as well as stupid, given the increasing likelihood of being found out. Better to be truthful and risk not getting shortlisted than lying, then being offered or starting the job and the lie being uncovered, where the career consequences can be so very serious.

## Implications

- Your CV needs to convey the best possible picture of you, but this does not mean misrepresentation.

- Where you are asked for actual information – date of birth, qualifications and so on – you must give them accurately.

- When you are asked to sign a declaration – for instance about county court judgements, your immigration status, nationality or your health record – you must be truthful.

- When an employer tells you as part of their paperwork in advance that they will be checking qualifications and employment record, believe it: this is not an empty threat and it is easy for them to do.

- It is not a good idea to let someone else write your CV for you, and most particularly, never let a recruitment agency rewrite it in a way that seriously misrepresents the truth. If challenged, they will disclaim all responsibility and you will be the one punished. Always check their 'improvements' and insist on corrections if what they produce is a material distortion.

- The more important some potentially compromising information is about you or your past, the more important it is to let the employer know at some point in the recruitment process, but not necessarily at the CV stage.

- Beware of apologizing unnecessarily for some problem in your CV: all this may do is draw the employer's attention to something they might otherwise have overlooked. For instance, if you have taken a career break to look after your children, you did this for excellent reasons and it is nothing to be ashamed of.

- When you are *not* asked for information that you think might be compromising, then there is an art in deciding whether or not to disclose it and when to disclose it.

You should also be aware of evidence that a degree of honesty about some potential gap, minor disadvantage or lack of experience actually creates a positive impression on an employer. It is disarming and creates an immediate impression of reliability and openness.

## Common CV embarrassments and how to get around them

Your task when you have some troubling feature in your career is to anticipate how the employer might respond, to face up to whatever that is and then to design your CV so that you minimize the damage.

I am going to start with the most mild risks and embarrassments, working through to the ones that potentially worry employers the most.

## Lacking qualifications that the employer has said are essential

*The employer's worry*: you are not intelligent enough to do the job, or your lack, for instance, of a graduate education will create limitations in your thinking.

*Your task*: to demonstrate that you have all the brain power needed for the role.

First you must judge how essential such apparently essential qualifications really are. If you need a licence to practise, for instance as a doctor, Anglican priest or pilot, then of course it is foolish to apply for such roles. When a job is based in Brussels and the employer asks for fluent French, then it is likely that fluent French is what is needed, though the degree of fluency may be open to interpretation. (Note that where languages are involved, employers virtually always hire specialist agencies to test and grade your accent, grammatical accuracy, fluency and comprehension.) But many jobs ask, for instance, for graduate qualifications when what is really meant is graduate-level capability. In such cases the employer is using the qualification as a simple screening process intended to deter people who may not have the intellectual capacity to do the job, so your task is to convince them that you do have such capacity.

Note also that the nature and class of your qualifications matter most when you are first entering the jobs market. They matter less and less as your career goes on because the skills and knowledge you have gathered from the various jobs you have done will be a lot more interesting and relevant than a qualification. When you are a youngster, the qualification is one of the few ways in which the employer can distinguish between you and other candidates who, to the naked eye, may look much the same.

### What to do

Check with the person handling the recruitment process and ask how vital it is to possess the qualification. Stress your ability to perform at the level the job needs. So, for instance, if you won a university place but did not complete the course, there could be good reasons for this which have nothing to do with your intellectual capability. Gaining university entry showed that you had the ability. Possession of a degree now cuts two ways. The high price of going to university is a deterrent to many potential students and so many degrees have been devalued as 'easy' (for instance, somewhat unfairly, Media Studies) or from universities that are far from being in the first rank, that it may indeed sometimes be better to demonstrate that while you were perfectly capable of getting a degree, you preferred to join the jobs market at 18 and have gained experience that actually puts you ahead of contemporaries who spent three years studying.

Consider:

- setting out the skills you have that match the qualification level required;

- emphasizing any training you have undertaken as a way of demonstrating your commitment to learning;

- ensuring that you list any further qualifications you have obtained;

- offering an explanation of why you missed out on the conventional qualifications.

Example: Martina is 34. Her education was compromised by civil war and political upheavals in her country of origin. She has completed two Open University courses that are relevant to the job for which she is now applying, as a development officer for a housing association, but this is far from being the degree that the employer has asked for.

Under the heading 'Qualifications', this is what Martina writes:

I left < name of country > at age 18, and was therefore unable to take up the university place I had been offered. On arrival in the UK as a refugee, my priority was to earn a living and later to support my family. However, I have been a committed learner, confident that I am a graduate-quality thinker, completing two self-funded Open University courses:

Welfare, Crime and Society, D208, 60 credit points, Distinction, < date >;

Introduction to Health and Social Care, K101, 60 credit points, Distinction, < date >.

Registered to begin Professional Diploma in Housing via distance learning with de Montfort University from September this year with the aim of eventually becoming a full member of the CIH, plus attending various courses ... [She then lists the courses.]

Variant: the employer has asked for a higher level of attainment or qualification than you have – for instance, passing exams without resits, getting a first, being awarded a degree from a 'Russell Group' institution (the 20 leading UK universities, sometimes compared to the 'Ivy League' colleges in the USA).

In this case, you have to gamble that there might not be enough applicants with the required level to create a decent shortlist, so you can deploy a variant of the advice above. State your actual qualifications and in the earlier part of your CV, stress the depth and range of your experience plus any evidence you can offer of relevant training courses, additional qualifications or other development you have undertaken.

## Your career has been a series of low-level, short-term jobs

This is a problem for people who have spent a few years mulling over what to do and have tided themselves over with a series of poorly paid jobs but now wish to enter the job market at a professional level.

*Alternative*: you have spent many years as a postgraduate student or 'travelling' and want a permanent job.

*The employer's worry*: you are immature and are unlikely to have the discipline to settle down to a proper job.

*Your task*: you must emphasize your maturity and your motivation to work.

This is increasingly a problem for inexperienced graduates, especially if they are young, but it can afflict mature students too. Most employers will understand that this is a structural problem created by recession, so it is less of an issue than in times when the economy is booming. They will also give you credit for having the energy and attack to find a job, even a lowly one, rather than sitting at home and living on benefits.

### What to do

This is a case for the opening paragraph or personal statement (Chapter 8) which describes your career to date and firmly states your job-seeking objective. The purpose is to help the employer understand that your travelling/compulsive studying/dossing-about days are over and that you are now seriously focused on a proper career.

Example: Daniel is a 40-year-old recent graduate in IT with a wife and two children. After an early career where he experimented somewhat unsuccessfully with running a variety of small businesses, he is looking for a better-paid permanent role. To fund his degree he has taken innumerable part-time and poorly paid jobs while his wife worked full time. This is what he writes at the top of his CV:

Recently graduated IT specialist with a 2.1 Honours degree from the University of East London, now seeking role managing a helpdesk or similar operation for a large organization. Innumerable part-time jobs in the service sector to fund my degree, as well as early experience as an entrepreneur, have given me sharp-end experience of customer service and why it matters as well as in-depth understanding of IT problems. My degree also included Business Administration and I believe I have a natural talent for management that enables me to lead an IT team with confidence.

## Other tactics

Emphasize:

- the parts of the previous roles which seem relevant to the new level of job – for instance: solving problems, dealing with difficult people, managing crises, handling money, organizing events and people;

- work and intern experience from your degree studies and what you learnt from these;

- the relevant knowledge which you acquired from your academic work;

- your personal qualities such as drive, enthusiasm and resilience.

## *Several recent short stays in many jobs*

*Employer's worry*: you are a flitter, hopping lightly from one job to another without commitment; there is some toxic reason behind the brevity of your tenure in the jobs.

*Your task*: reassure the employer that none of the above is true.

## What to do

- Where you have undertaken the work on an agreed temporary basis, say so. Temp, project-based and interim work are now common career patterns and most employers will understand this.

- Use the skills-based format rather than the chronological career history format (page 115) and emphasize the breadth of your skills.

- Cluster a period of work which involved several projects by putting them under one heading.

- Although normally it is not good practice to give a reason for leaving a job, if your job changes were as a result of contraction in the market, bankruptcy or the retirement of the owner, say so.

- Give dates as years rather than months, though note that sometimes employers insist on month details and in some careers – eg medicine – it is obligatory.

- Prepare a convincing answer to potential challenges about job-hopping for the interview.

## *Long stay in one job or organization*

*The employer's worry:* long stayers lack the gumption to take risks and have become too institutionalized in one organization to adapt to another.

*Your task:* build a more detailed picture of your long-stay career; emphasize the transferability of your skills and experience.

This matters less to employers than many candidates believe. Until comparatively recently it was the norm to be a long stayer and there are still large organizations where it is possible to enjoy an entire and fulfilling career. However, it would be rare to stay in literally the same job for decades and most long stayers have found themselves in large organizations where there is plenty of scope for variety of work – and this is probably what has kept them there. If this applies to you, you will have moved around at least a little, have been promoted a few times and have been involved in a number of different roles. Sometimes, although the job title stays the same, the role has in fact been different.

## What to do

- Treat your long stay exactly as if your different roles and responsibilities have been different jobs. In other words, write the CV as if the fact that they are all in one organization is irrelevant. List the job titles, roles and achievements with dates under separate headings.

- Long stayers often forget how thoroughly they have absorbed the organization's culture and draft a CV that would be fine for internal consumption but that makes absolutely no sense to anyone on the outside. Be careful to remove all acronyms and other organization-specific jargon and details of job grades from your CV. Give the draft to a total outsider to check whether they understand it.

- Essential: make it easy for the employer to see that you have developed and grown. Emphasize the way you have added to your accomplishments as your career went on. If you are that rare person, someone who has literally been in the same job, then list the different projects for which you have had responsibility.

Example: Deri was a radio producer for 15 years, quietly enjoying what he regarded as fulfilling work and with little ambition to progress to a managerial role. A cost-cutting exercise meant the loss of his job. He had had one promotion to senior producer but all this really meant was recognition for long service and getting more money for doing the same work. In drafting his CV, Deri proudly listed all the high-profile programmes on which he had worked, starting with the most recent and working backwards, and emphasized his role in developing innovative programmes, working successfully with household-name presenters and winning two highly respected awards for his work.

## You are over-qualified for the job

*Employer's worry*: you are desperate; you won't stay; you are running away from something; you could cause trouble by being annoyingly bossy or patronizing.

*Your task*: stress the close match of your skills to the job; downplay the glories of your career.

There are many excellent reasons for downsizing a career. Of course, it may indeed be the case that you have been made redundant and, given the shortage of jobs, that there are no comparable jobs for which you could apply. Or it may be that, if you are a recent immigrant, the qualifications you obtained in your country of origin are not recognized in the UK. Far more commonly with my own clients, they have decided that they want jobs where it is possible to live a simpler and more rounded life. Such people are not money oriented and have often passed through some crisis such as a bereavement where they have jerked themselves awake to their real priorities and have decided to take a measured decision.

## What to do

- Contact the hiring manager or HR person verbally before submitting your CV and in discussing your interest in the role, give a brief, positive and plausible account of your reasons for making the change so that you have prepared the ground for your CV and established that the employer would be interested in receiving an application from you.

- Use the skills-based format for page 1 of your CV, working steadily through the skills and qualities the employer lists.

- Downplay the responsibilities associated with your previously glossy job.

- Keep the career history part of the CV brief.

- Never include your previous salary (this is a general rule anyway – see page 73).

Example: Diana was chief operations officer for a large company. She described herself to me as 'a member of the sandwich generation', with responsibility for elderly parents as well as being a single parent to her own teenage children. She earned enough money to pay for good-quality care for her parents but her life was stressful: rushing between meetings, working long hours and travelling out of the UK an average of 50 days a year. After a crisis over the care of her parents, she decided to look for a less pressured job, ideally the same type of role but in a smaller organization and one that would in all probability pay considerably less than her current job but that would allow her to spend more time with her parents and children. She spotted an ideal role that was locally based, a job that would enable her to be at work in a few minutes, to leave promptly at 6 pm and that would still be an interesting way to earn a living. The salary was less than half the sum she was then paid. Diana called the CEO of the organization and in the first few moments of the conversation explained her skills and experience, quickly following this with an explanation of why she was attracted to the role, emphasizing the attraction of having more direct control over her work and the challenge of helping a company grow. When finally asked about her salary and, reasonably, why she would be prepared to take such a major cut, she explained that money was not and never had been her main motivator, that she enjoyed her job but had recently taken stock of her life and was making a cool and considered decision. Diana submitted her CV, subtly downplaying her previous responsibilities and emphasizing her functional skills, made the shortlist and was offered the job, with both sides feeling lucky.

## Age: too old?

*Employer's worry*: you are stuck in your ways, or lack the essential skills that a younger person would automatically have.

*Your task*: demonstrate your vigour and the up-to-date nature of your thinking.

The age at which you can feel disadvantaged by being 'too old' varies hugely from one job and sector to another. A professional footballer is old at 30. A US president is young at 40 and evidently (Ronald Reagan) not too old at 77. A police officer can retire at 50, and consider themselves too old to run about after street criminals, but a chief constable can continue until 65. Some of the world's greatest conductors are no longer young – at one concert I watched André Previn, then in his 80s, totter onto the stage with the aid of a helper and proceed to do a magnificent job with the orchestra, conducting while sitting down.

### What to do

- Be sensible about applying for jobs where there is overt prejudice about age, but also be aware that since 2006, with additions in 2010, UK legislation protects you against discrimination on grounds of age.

- See your age as an advantage and emphasize the benefits of your wisdom and experience. As Ronald Reagan said when campaigning for re-election: 'I am not going to make age an issue of this campaign. I am not going to exploit, for political purposes, my opponent's youth and inexperience.' His opponent, Walter Mondale, was 56 at the time.

- In writing a personal profile, use words like energetic, enthusiastic, vigorous, driven, ambitious.

- In describing your achievements and roles, ensure that you emphasize the energy you have brought to your work.

- Draw examples of your experience and achievements from your most recent roles.

- Include IT skills and give details of packages you can use confidently.

- Don't give your date of birth on the CV unless specifically asked for it.

- Take especial care with the appearance of your CV, giving it a contemporary look.

- When you get to the interview, make sure that your appearance is up to date in every way. If you have any doubts about this, ask a younger friend who can be trusted to be ruthlessly frank – and act on any advice they offer, for instance about hair, accessories, make-up and clothing.

## Too young

*Employer's worry*: youth = inexperience; you are not ready for the responsibility.

*Your task*: demonstrate your maturity.

Age discrimination can work both ways and it is just as maddening to be rejected for a job on grounds of youth as it is to be rejected on grounds of being too old. Again, be sensible. If the employer states clearly that they are looking for a minimum of five years' experience of a specific type and you have only one, it is unlikely that your application will be taken seriously.

Craft your CV using the skills-based rather than the chronological format (page 115).

Emphasize the skills that will lend you gravitas – for instance, using words like leading, managing, developing, producing (see page 81 for more suggestions).

## Career gaps

Increasingly, people do have gaps in their career histories and how you deal with them will depend on what they are.

## What to do

Where you have this kind of career gap, the best strategies are these:

- Avoid apologizing or over-explaining – leave any explanations for the interview; be brief and factual.

- Where you have taken time out to have a sabbatical, raise a child, care for an elderly parent, get a qualification, travel, then these are not gaps in any real sense as all will have been experiences from which you can develop, and should be put forward on your CV as such.

- Minimize the space you allot to the gap in your CV or even to take the risk of omitting it and hoping the employer won't notice.

- Accept that the longer ago such a gap is, the less it will matter to the employer.

- Make sure you mention any refresher or other training courses that you have undertaken during the career break.

- Stress your knowledge of trends in the organization or sector through what you say in the covering letter.

Examples: Belinda has been out of the paid job market for 10 years. In the career history section of her CV she ends it with:

< date > to < date >: Full-time parent to my three daughters.

In the skills section of her CV she describes the organizing skills she has acquired during her parenting role, emphasizing her sense of responsibility and reliability.

Gilles and his girlfriend resigned from their jobs in their middle twenties to take a year out to travel, as neither had had the privilege of a gap year as students. They wanted to see the world before settling down to marriage and children. Gilles puts it like this on his CV:

< date > to < date >: A one-year world-travel project. Task: go round the world on a total budget of £5,000 with my partner. Visited 14 countries, learnt Spanish, part-funded trip through photography and teaching English.

## Illness and disability

Gaps caused by ill health are a bigger problem. One recent survey revealed what we all suspect to be true, that roughly one-third of employers routinely reject anyone who has had a period on disability benefits and is now trying to return to work. Here the employer's worry is that your illness was a fiction covering laziness or that the illness will return; that poor health means you will be less likely to work hard or will need a lot of time off for treatment. The Equality Act of 2010 made it harder for employers to act out of prejudice here, but common sense suggests that this will not prevent them from trying.

Be sensible. Don't apply for a job which you can see would demand physical or mental effort which you could not make. If the job states clearly that you need to be capable of walking up to 10 miles a day and you have mobility problems, this is not the job for you. In my time as a BBC producer and when people were just beginning to think about the implications of the BBC's equal opportunities policy, I overheard a solemn discussion about whether a blind colleague could become a television producer. However much one would wish to give someone with a disability every chance, this was clearly one job he simply could not do.

### What to do

If the gap in your CV is caused by ill health, you might try:

- Listing your career before and after the gap and hoping that the employer will not notice.

- Giving a brief factual explanation and emphasizing your return to full health, if this is indeed the case.

- Listing the dates during which you were ill but labelling them 'Illness and complete recovery'.

Example: Thalia is 29. Before she had completed her second year as a qualified doctor she was involved in a serious road accident which she was lucky to survive. She has had to review her career, and her former plan to train as an accident and emergency specialist is no longer sensible or possible. Treatment has been lengthy but her recovery has progressed to the point where she can walk with the aid of only one stick and no longer needs painkillers to get through her day. She is now training as a GP. In crafting her CV she writes:

< date > to < date > [a two-year period]: Major surgery and recuperation. Involved in hit-and-run accident in May < date >, resulting in extensive trauma: pelvic and chest surgery plus bone reconstruction in both legs. Now fully recovered, though with some impaired mobility.

If you need special equipment or help with access because you have a mobility or sensory problem, the way to reveal this is on a piece-by-piece basis, and after you have been offered the job, not as a set of aggressive demands on your CV ('I know my rights!'). The Equalities and Human Rights Commission website, www.equalityhumanrights.com, offers up-to-date information on the law.

Make sure that when you appear at the interview you look lively and full of energy.

## Redundancy or a period of unemployment

*Employer's worry*: you have lost the habit of work; you lost your job for some sinister reason. The longer the period of unemployment, the more the employer worries about it.

*Your task*: emphasizing your skills and accomplishments.

Depending on where you live and what your previous work has been, you may find employers tolerant – and unworried – by a period of unemployment. For instance, if you live in an area where whole swathes of work have disappeared because whole industries have died, then unemployment might, sadly, be the norm. If you live in places like London and the South East where work is always available, even if poorly paid and unpleasant, the employer may wonder why you have not taken it.

### What to do

- The skills-based CV (page 115) is a better bet than the chronological CV, especially if you have had more than one period of unemployment.

- Describing the period of unemployment as freelance or consultancy work is a good way of conveying that you have been busy and productive – as long as this is true. At the interview, expect to be probed about how real such freelance work has been, so you need to be able to give convincing examples of projects and be able to name your clients.

- Making the most of any temporary work, even if in reality it has been badly paid and sporadic.

Example: Alex is 30 and comes from a London Turkish family. He lost his junior manager job when his firm restructured but the reality is that he was the obvious candidate for cuts because of his poor timekeeping, the sluggishness caused by his obesity, and a drinking problem that meant too many severe hangovers too frequently. He has been out of work for two years. After a year of feeling sorry for himself and lurking upstairs at his parents' home, he is now a reformed character: has lost five stone in weight, goes to the reasonably priced local authority gym several times a week, looks slim, fit and healthy and is eager to find work. He is interested in food and wants to restart with a career in the hospitality sector without having to be at the bottom of the heap with the most unpleasant and worst-paid work. In his CV he lists some of the many ways that cash-in-hand jobs have kept him going, without describing them as such. For instance, he turns distributing leaflets and being a 'greeter' for his uncle's Turkish restaurant into 'restaurant sales and customer care'; he turns helping a friend run his building business into 'freelance designing, painting and decorating'; he turns working as a food preparer and waiter for another uncle who has a successful catering business into 'catering assistant and commis chef'; his interest in cooking means he has dabbled with the idea of making his ideas known to a wider public and he turns this into 'recipe development and writing the first draft of a cookery book'. None of this is untrue, it gives good clues to his genuine interests and it sounds a great deal better than implying he has just sat at home living miserably on the jobseeker's allowance.

This is one place where you might consider stating the reason for leaving a job, by briefly describing what happened, assuming that it was the job that was terminated, not you. Reflect this in how you write about it and keep it short and simple – for example, write something like 'Company was restructured and post was made redundant.' This is always a better way to phrase it than 'I was made redundant.' Depending on the circumstances, you might also consider adding a few more explanatory words which put the emphasis on the company rather than on you. For instance, 'Economic downturn pushed the company into receivership and the job disappeared.'

Give due emphasis to any voluntary work that has occupied you during the period of unemployment.

Example: Bradley had left a well-paid role in an oil company after a long series of disputes with his boss. At 52, he was realistic about the low chances of getting another six-figure-plus salary but his 'compromise agreement' gave him enough money to sit out up to a year of unemployment while he thought carefully about what to do next. He knew that taking his time to find another role could look suspicious to employers and he also dreaded spending too much time brooding unproductively, so he undertook several volunteer roles, all of which involved initiating, leading and organizing: starting up a both-sexes under-eights rugby club for his village and for which he was the coach; becoming a parent governor of his local school and leading their fundraising activities; taking on a churchwarden and lay-reader role in his church and standing in for the vicar on a regular basis; becoming treasurer in the village 'AmDram' group. He gave these activities a prominent role in his CV because they conveyed, quite correctly, that he was an active, go-getting person who could make things happen.

## You were dismissed from your last job

*Employer's worry*: you were sacked for good reason.

*Your task*: to avoid or postpone revealing this, especially at the CV stage.

Employment legislation is designed to protect employees from unreasonable employer behaviour and this includes what was all too possible in the bad old days: sacking an employee on a whim. So although this is good news for most employees, it is bad news for anyone who is actually sacked, as all potential future employers will know that there must have been a convincing reason for it. This will vary on a spectrum from mild incompetence sustained over a long period and which gradually became too much for the employer to bear, to gross misconduct – for instance, sexual or racial abuse, stealing and any behaviour which puts others in danger.

Do not reveal this reason for leaving on your CV if you possibly can. It is also unwise whether at CV or at interview stage to appear to blame the previous employer or to sound bitter and angry. Any future employer will immediately think, 'If this person is saying this about that employer, then the chances are that they'll soon be saying the same about me.' Equally, who wants a resentful employee, still obsessed with the injustices of the past? At the interview, keep any explanations brief and factual. Wherever possible, emphasize the two-way nature of the agreement to part. Where leaving your last job was caused by gross misconduct, it is often impossible to conceal and if confronted, the best tactic is to talk candidly, straightforwardly and briefly about how much you have learnt from your mistake. Where any such leaving is in the past, and has been followed by several years of successful employment, it is unlikely that it will be a problem.

## A criminal conviction; a prison sentence

*Employer's worry*: you will reoffend.

*Your task*: do not disclose any conviction on your CV unless specifically asked.

Sentencing is intended, at least partially, to reform the offender. But the very fact of the conviction, especially if it has involved a custodial sentence, makes it many times more difficult for the person to get back into mainstream society, thus making it more likely that they will reoffend. Employer prejudice is understandable even if often an exaggerated response and is more likely to kick in if you are applying for exactly the same kind of job that provided temptation in the past – for instance, someone with a conviction for embezzlement is unlikely to get a job as an accountant.

This is the legal situation: depending on whether sentences are 'spent' or 'unspent', under the Rehabilitation of Offenders Act 1974, ex-offenders, including ex-prisoners, are only obliged to disclose criminal records if asked to do so by employers. If they are not asked, or if they are asked but do not answer the question (ie do not lie as such) they commit no offence under the Fraud Act. It follows that ex-offenders do not have to disclose their offences on CVs because by their very nature employers are not asking them for disclosure. If there are gaps in the CV because the person has served a long period of imprisonment, the onus is on prospective employers to identify those gaps and perhaps interrogate the applicant at interview about them. If the applicant fills those gaps in their CV with phrases like 'not in work', they are not lying (ie committing fraud) and the onus remains on the employer to ask them why they were not in work. For certain kinds of work – for instance, with children or other vulnerable groups – the Rehabilitation of Offenders Act does not apply and checks will be made with the Criminal Records Bureau. All convictions have to be disclosed for these jobs, including those considered to be 'spent'.

In general it is best to omit any conviction or custodial sentence from a CV and only to disclose it, if you have to, verbally, emphasizing that you have paid your debt to society and are now a reformed character. Depending on the job and sector where you wish to work, you may also wish to take inspiration from people like Erwin James, imprisoned for murder and now a writer, and Jonathan Aitken, a high-profile politician whose career crashed when he was imprisoned for perjury but who has since reinvented himself as a speaker and prison reformer. Both these men have made a virtue out of talking openly and maturely about their crimes. There are several organizations which exist to help ex-offenders. The leading one is NACRO (www.nacro.org.uk). They run a helpline, offer a useful leaflet and have innumerable other services which include information on jobseeking.

# THE CV SECTION

In this section of the book there are six CVs of different types, representing typical career challenges. The details given at the end of the chapter will allow you to view these CVs and eight others in finished form as online PDFs. The purpose of these samples is to show how a complete CV looks, using different styles and approaches. Most are based on real-life CVs, details disguised, with the person's consent. Some are blends of several actual CVs and some are fictionalized, invented to demonstrate particular points.

None of these CVs is intended to offer you a perfect fit that you can lift straight out and use. This is because there is no true shortcut to creating the CV that will be precisely right for you. You are the only person who can do this. However, in scanning these CV examples, you can look at how the people concerned have:

- chosen layout and typeface. There will be some that appeal to you more than others and which you can use as inspiration for your own CV.

- solved particular problems in presenting their careers and lives, emphasizing strong points and minimizing weak ones.

- used 'CV language' to create a document with impact.

- selected one format rather than another.

- broken some of the classic 'rules' of CV writing – and why.

The idea is for you to judge for yourself how far these CVs do the job for which they were intended and to give you a kick start in writing your own.

# Manager NHS

Although Jane's CV may look as if it is only suitable as a template for another NHS senior manager, in fact it could form the basis of any managerial job, with different evidence, of course, but the headings are the competencies needed for most managerial work.

Jane is the chief executive of a medium-sized NHS hospital and is looking specifically for a bigger hospital, probably a teaching Trust. She is aware that her own hospital is a target for merger and wants to change jobs before this happens. Ideally she wants to stay in the hospital sector of the NHS or would consider a move to local government, central government or to the private health sector where her experience would serve her well. She has emphasised her leadership and managerial achievements. Her aim is to give the message to any potential employer that she is a fearless exponent of change with a strong track record of delivering on targets. Any job for which she applies will probably have headhunter involvement.

Jane has taken the calculated risk of extending her CV to three A4 pages to allow for a further emphasis on her skills, this time using the space to describe her management style – and in a more informal way than she has used on the first two pages, for instance using the first person. She could make a decision later to remove this, if she wished – or to use it in the covering letter. It will depend on the advice she gets from the headhunter in relation to any specific job.

---

Page 1 of 3

Jane Morgan
46 St Augustine Rd
Kingston on Thames
KT4 9QT
M: 07863 996543        E: JMorgan5.home@orange.co.uk

---

*EMPLOYMENT HISTORY*

**2006–present**

**Chief Executive, Beckford and Wallington NHS Foundation Trust**

*Achievements*

- *Managing change*: Led difficult merger between previous two hospitals. Strategy concentrated on creating a patient-led culture. Staff morale is high with year-on-year improvements in staff survey; sickness absence reduced from 10% to 5%.

- *Financial management*: Commissioned new information systems for tight cost control, now on target for a zero deficit and have managed within budget for last two years. Reduced overhead costs by 30% by rationalizing property portfolio. Reduced operating costs by 25% by initiating process reviews mapping patient pathway.
- *Strategic leadership*: Developed new strategy, clarifying what services we are in (and not in); e.g. that we are in rheumatology, orthopaedics and cancer services; diminishing importance given to elderly services because they will be developed by the XX Trust [a neighbouring hospital].
- *Quality assurance*: Led the process of tougher clinical governance in the Trust with full involvement of clinical staff. Excellent reports from Care Quality Commission.
- *Team leadership*: Have created strong, flexible team capable of responding swiftly to both strategic and operational issues. Have retained the services of a talented group in face of competition from elsewhere.
- *Collaborative working*: generated strong relationships with local authorities plus most of leading voluntary agencies. For past two years Trust has coped well with winter pressures – no 'patients on trolleys' stories in the local press and a confident approach from staff, thanks to increased cooperation with GPs and community nursing services.
- *Results focus*: We are on target to reduce our lists to below the national average.
- *Operational management*: Developed constructive ways to manage the interface between huge orthopaedic workload and the need to admit emergencies in winter.
- *Patient experience*: Commissioned clinician-led review of all acute services, streamlining and shortening distressing delays. Most recent Patient Satisfaction Survey shows 85% of patients believe they received 'outstanding' or 'very good' care.

## 2000–2006

### Director of Operations, Dereham NHS trust

Dereham is an acute hospital with 450 beds. It is the major accident and emergency trauma centre for North West Norfolk, a Calman Cancer Centre and also has neurology, paediatric, maternity and obstetric services.

*Achievements*

- Improved waiting times, average 16 weeks, bringing them to one of lowest in UK.
- Introduced tight financial management resulting in low running costs and the reduction of deficit to zero.
- Led major, innovative capital developments achieved within normal NHS guidelines – e.g. patient dining rooms, ensuite rooms, an ambience of dignity and respect for patients.
- Achieved collaborative working with sister Trust, the N & N in Norwich, avoiding pointless competitiveness.
- Created a model Calman–Hine Cancer Centre featuring hospice and patient information centre.

- Developed new risk management system.
- Led the achievement of Investors in People accreditation.
- Secured voluntary donations of £3m, enabling us to establish field-leading endoscopy and diabetes day units and pioneering outpatient facilities.

## EARLIER CAREER

1995–2000 Unit General Manager, City and East Norfolk Health Authority

1984–1986 Unit General Manager, Bloomsbury Health Authority

1993–1995 Team Leader, Surrey County Council Social Services

1990–1993 Children and Families Social Worker

## SKILLS AND QUALITIES

*Strategic thinking*: My track record demonstrates that I have had to use high-quality strategic thinking, especially in my last two posts. I am a creative thinker with an eye to the longer-term future. I believe in living with ambiguity and in using a *both/and* approach rather than the limitations of *either/or*.

*Personal resilience*: I am a hard and conscientious worker who still regards her personal life as important. My approach is to tackle what is important rather than what is urgent. This includes a proper balance between my work and private lives, which protects me from stress.

*Leadership*: My approach is to involve, to challenge and to support, not just with my immediate team but with as many people in the whole organization as possible. I have successfully developed a number of innovative ways of doing this.

*Developing and coaching*: My aim is always to develop and coach through feedback, challenge and support rather than to command and control. The result is empowered teams who get on with their own jobs rather than asking me to do theirs. At the same time, I demand – and get – high standards, relying on this rather than expecting any formal performance management system to achieve it for me.

*Financial management*: I am keenly interested in financial results, am numerate and interested in robust financial models which help get the most out of limited resources.

*Quality*: Clinical and other kinds of audit are critical to the success of a modern NHS. The only way to do this satisfactorily is to involve the clinicians in genuine leadership and management. This is a hard task, but I have now achieved it in two Trusts.

*Influencing*: I rely on personal power, not position power, to achieve what I believe needs to be done. My approach is collaborative and the excellent relationships I have achieved with other NHS and local authority chief executives are proof of this.

## INTERESTS

Walking in the Lake District; Latin American dance; running; 20th-century history; reading and writing poetry.

## QUALIFICATIONS

MBA: Cranfield Institute of Technology, 2000
CQSW: 1988
BA, Hons: University of Bristol, History, 2.1, 1986

# Postgraduate with little work experience

This example of a one-page CV shows how powerful a carefully targeted approach can be, even when you are at the absolute beginning of a career and without either a great deal of employment experience or brilliant A level results. Matthew has decided that he wants a City or consulting career and has stripped down his CV to the essentials that will catch the eye of a graduate recruiter in these fields, even in times when such jobs are scarce and competition fierce. His school results look mediocre (and he might do better to omit them in future CVs) but his degree from a first-rate university and his exposure to German language and culture suggest an international outlook. His MA in War Studies, again from an impressive university, and his dissertation on a challenging internationally relevant subject suggest a lively, analytical mind. His employment experience is extremely limited but he has given a flavour of his willingness to plunge into new worlds confidently and to get results. It is clear from his personal interests that he has devoted time to political and social concerns. He has used a classic typeface: Times New Roman. Note that he has omitted the humble 'McJobs' that it is likely he did during vacations. This is a risk but it has paid off here. The real-life CV on which this version is based quickly earned its writer innumerable offers of interviews for jobs with good salaries, and therefore the portal to a flourishing career in his chosen sector.

---

Page 1 of 2

Matthew Freeman
26 St Andrews Rd
Leatherhead, KT52 6TM
Matthewfreeman88@yahoo.co.uk (+44) 07865 623451

**Bright, presentable International Relations postgraduate with fluent German, good knowledge of emerging markets, with banking and marketing experience.**

## EMPLOYMENT

*Private Banking*

*July 2009 NatWest Private Banking, Bristol*
Internship involved working for a variety of private bankers, learning about the role of Relationship Managers and sales executives. Developed teamwork and leadership skills as part of the winning group in a competition involving a presentation to NatWest executives as a pitch to win funds for a charity.

*Public Relations and Advertising*

*Winter 2009–2010 PCMB Advertising, London*
As an Account Executive worked on variety of accounts including Midland Trains and FastGov, developing copywriting, account management and client relationship skills. Acted as liaison between creative team, client and senior management.

*Summer 2008 Singleton Public Relations, London*
Developed interpersonal and negotiation skills as Account Executive. Had daily contact with clients, pitching to journalists, writing press releases, liaising with media, managing databases and organizing press conferences. Predominantly worked on the London Olympics Account and also for clients such as Mitre & McGovern plc.

## EDUCATION

*2010–2011 Kings College London, War Studies Department, MA International Relations: Merit*
Research interests: South Asian security; interplay of social, economic, political and cultural factors; how this impacts on the West.
Dissertation: India's relations with the USA, US foreign policies in India – success and failure – nature of India's ambitions in the world and the economic and security implications which result.

*2005–2008 University College, London. BA German and History, 2.1*
Spent third year working as teaching assistant in German school.
Dissertation: Macro-economics and the German economy 2000–2005.

*2000–2005 Smithson School, London.*
A levels: A, B, B; GCSEs: 2 As, 4 Bs and 3 Cs

## OTHER SKILLS
German language fluency, Level 9 International Certificate. Studying for Investment Management Certificate. Excellent computer skills in Word, Excel, PowerPoint.

## INTERESTS
Charity work: volunteer for Future Hope, teaching English to street children in Kolkata. Politics: volunteered to work for local Conservative candidate in run-up to 2010 election. Team sports: captained school and college tennis 1st teams. Other interests: travel photography, club squash player, sprinting, competitive cycling, skiing.

# Salesperson to manager

James has now been in estate agency work for six years and has had fast promotion because he can sell property when colleagues struggle. When his boss had a breakdown and went off sick for six months, James stood in for him and realized that he loved running a sales team. He feels he is a natural leader. Now he's looking for a new job as a sales manager. He urgently needs to earn more, buy or rent his own flat and the job needs to be in Belfast or Dublin because of his personal circumstances.

James's CV makes the most of his experience in his current role as a way of countering his relative youth and emphasizes the unusual breadth of his successes and innovations for one so young. For the same reason he has chosen Garamond, a somewhat sober typeface, to give an impression of maturity. He has given his driving licence status when normally you would omit this, but in his profession it is important and employers request it. Similarly, you always need to hesitate before including training courses in a CV but in James's case it is worthwhile as it shows his commitment to his own development and the choice of courses is interesting. An employer looking for someone professionally interested in leadership would also see that James has invested considerable amounts of time, and possibly his own money, in his personal development – for instance with his post-graduate diploma in management.

James has registered with several recruitment agencies specializing in sales roles and will also network vigorously, knowing that the most likely way a new job will come his way is through personal contact.

---

Page 1 of 3

James S. Smith
582 Lisburn Park Rd
Belfast
BT15 8OQ

Telephone 02890 89 5162    Email JamesSSmith5.belfast. home@bluesky.com

---

A confident senior sales negotiator with 6 years' enjoyable and productive experience in estate agency. Outstanding sales success, consistently delivering above targets, popular with vendors, purchasers and colleagues; committed to improving the image of the profession – selling property in a way which meets needs of both buyer and seller and acting with integrity at all times. Developer of innovative and successful web-based approaches to marketing and client management. NLP Master Practitioner. Now looking for a role as sales manager in Belfast or Dublin to sell commercial or residential property and to lead a team hungry for results.

## ACHIEVEMENTS AND CAREER

**Senior Negotiator, Emerson Property, Belfast, 2008 – present**

Handling all aspects of residential property sales; managing own client list; dealing with enquiries; liaising with solicitors and mortgage brokers.

Won company award as Sales Negotiator of the Year, 2010. Exceeded monthly targets every month in 2011 and increased sales revenue by 20%.

Developed successful new strategy for advertising campaign in local press and web which resulted in doubling number of initial enquiries. Website traffic tripled after making business case for and then implementing improved picture quality, more interesting copy and introducing video.

Developed improved software to track sales and trigger automatic follow-ups to investigate delays.

Coached vendors in: radical ways to improve first impressions of their property; how to price realistically in a downturned market.

Created strong relationships with network of lawyers, surveyors, valuers and mortgage brokers to reduce sales cycle time from offer to contract and completion.

Initiated method of analysing and then acting on client segmentation and profiles to guide marketing policy.

Inducted and trained junior staff.

Managed budgets and forecasting, deputizing for boss.

Gave presentations to colleagues at other branches, briefing them on our methods.

Stood in for manager when he was off sick for a 6-month period. Handled staff appraisals, dealt with motivating and rebuilding a team demoralized by exceptionally difficult trading conditions.

**Sales negotiator, TQZ Property, 12 Claremont St, London W1 2006–2008**

Handled all aspects of property selling, specializing in commercial property. Achieved all sales targets. Learnt to work under pressure at this premier agency. Made initial visits to properties, drew up paperwork and wrote advertisements. Conducted initial presentation of property to potential buyers and followed up offers; carried through negotiations.

## EARLIER CAREER

**Trainee sales negotiator, Foxtons, Kensington, London 2005–2006**

**Sales assistant, House of Fraser, Menswear Department, Oxford St, London 2004–2005**

**Variety of temporary jobs including McDonald's, bar and restaurant work 2003–2004**

**Travelling in Australia, Singapore and New Zealand 2002–2003**

**QUALIFICATIONS**

University of Ulster; BSc Business 2.2; 2002

Postgraduate Diploma in Management Studies; London Metropolitan University, 2008

NLP Master Practitioner; NLP Academy 2009; trained with John Grinder, one of the founders of NLP

**PROFESSIONAL DEVELOPMENT**

Have attended innumerable courses including:

Excellence in selling

Managing difficult clients

Mediating in disputes (one-term evening course)

Business development

Legal aspects of estate agency (modular course over a year)

Finance for non-financial managers

**DRIVING LICENCE**

Full, clean licence

**PERSONAL**

Triathlete; playing rugby; qualified rugby coach and referee; travelling to far-flung places.

# IT expert to salaried job

Stepan is Bulgarian and is part of the trend that brings talented East Europeans to the UK. He has had a number of jobs with companies supplying IT services or working on helpdesks. His last job ended when the company went into administration. He has found self-employment bleak and lonely as he is not a natural self-promoter. He is now looking for a salaried job.

He knows that any British employer will wonder about his command of English, so he mentions the language study he did in Scotland. He is multilingual and this will be an advantage in any company trading with the former Soviet Union. Stepan has a British wife. Normally you do not need to mention your marital status but Stepan does so because he wishes to emphasize the stability of his current situation and for the same reason he mentions that he is applying for British citizenship as he is determined to make the UK his permanent home.

IT specialists frequently fail to mention their so-called 'soft skills' but in any customer-facing role this will be important. This is why Stepan mentions his abilities here, knowing that this will give him an edge over competitors.

Stepan Botev
16 Kings Cross Rd
London
E15 6TF
07757 689 724 stepan@ITserve.com

*Objective*: to contribute first-class IT technical skills in a customer service company in the London or Greater London area.

*Profile*: a highly qualified IT professional with 7 years' experience in customer-facing IT. Enjoys problem solving; friendly, persistent. Can teach customers how to use software. Up to date in website development and maintenance. Hard-working, flexible; fluent in English, Russian and Bulgarian.

## EMPLOYMENT HISTORY

*Feb 2009 – present: self-employed*
IT engineer working on PC maintenance and repair for range of East London small business and individual customers, solving hardware and software problems.

*Jan 2005 – Feb 2009: Pentagonal IT Ltd – engineer*
Created custom-built computers for home and small business customers.
Built specialist servers.
Networking support for home and commercial customers, wired and wireless.
Repaired and replaced laptop hardware.
Installed CCTV systems.
Dealt with PDAs, IPAQs, Palm OS.

*Dec 2003 – Jan 2005: Technical support analyst, Computer Technologies Ltd, Edinburgh*
Restructured and maintained company's website.
Configured, rolling out and troubleshooting desktop and server systems.
Transferred complex data between servers in multiple-domain controllers network.
Successfully relocated company's IT infrastructure to new premises with minimum downtime.
Solved technical problems for users re networking, servers, hard drives, wireless points, back-up, etc.

*2004 – 2005: Software developer, Technocomp Sofia*
C# programming languages; developed MS SQL and MySQL databases for small business clients.

## TECHNICAL SKILLS – TROUBLESHOOTING AND MAINTENANCE FOR:
Windows: 2000/XP/Server2003
Active Directory 2003
MS Office: all applications
Exchange Server 2003
VMware: workstation/server
Networking: TCP/IP. IPX/SPX, NetBIOS
Linux: RHEL -4, Ubuntu 6, 7, 8
Data back-up and recovery.

*CUSTOMER-HANDLING SKILLS:*

Pleasant, polite manner with customers.

Keep customers informed of unavoidable delays in servicing their equipment.

Patience; able to deal successfully with anxious or angry customers.

Able to teach customers more effective use of their software.

*QUALIFICATIONS*

2006 NCC International Advanced Diploma in Computer Studies, London Computer College, Holborn

2003 NCC International Diploma in Computer Studies, BMC College, Edinburgh

2004 Technical University of Sofia. Honours Degree in Business Studies and Computing, 1st class

*ADDITIONAL INFORMATION*

Undertook intensive English course while in Edinburgh. Speak fluent English, Bulgarian and Russian, reasonable French. Private interests include repairing antique watches, playing and watching football, French 'noir' films.

Married. Currently applying for UK citizenship.

# Job hopper

Kayleigh left school at 18 with unimpressive A level results. She was not interested in university but had no clear idea about what she wanted to do instead. As the only one of her friends without higher education qualifications she is seeing them overtake her in income and job satisfaction. The truth is that until recently she has been a somewhat unfocused job hopper, working to live rather than living to work, holding a series of low-paid jobs with little prospect of promotion.

Now at 29 with a partner and with a mortgage to feed, she has decided to get a grip on her career and to go full-out for a job selling cosmetics in a department store or working as the in-house therapist at a gym or spa as a prelude to specializing in skin care and make-up – and even, eventually, to running her own business.

Kayleigh's younger sister has a large 'port wine stain' facial birthmark and Kayleigh has been aware of how much this has affected her sister's life and confidence. This is what encouraged her to learn camouflage techniques as part of the portfolio of skills and experience she can now offer.

She scraped together the money for a part-time NVQ Beauty Therapy course at her local college and managed to talk her way into heavily subsidized places on two other relevant short courses. Showing that she has stuck at this at this will impress any future employer but she will still have to demonstrate that her job-hopping days are over.

Kayleigh has opted for a version of the skills-based CV, headed by an informally written profile and a statement of her career objective. In reality her CV is a list of the skills she has acquired on her Beauty Therapy course – and note that she has clustered the part-time and contract jobs together to minimize the reality of a rackety earlier career when she skated precariously from one short-term and unsatisfying low-paid job to another. She has not given details of her A level grades and hopes that any interviewer will not enquire too closely since two Es do not look good.

---

### Kayleigh Simeon
25 Middleton St, Exeter, EX16 8NU
07796 573433 email Kayleighsi@googlemail.com

---

Qualified Beauty Therapist, distinction in all modules at NVQ Level 2, special interests in colour and style in clothing and make-up and also in depilation of all sorts. Committed to the difference that wonderful make-up and hair can make to appearance and confidence. Conscientious, friendly and highly client focused, excellent selling skills. Now seeks full-time employment in a cosmetics department or health spa.

### SKILLS AND QUALITIES

- High standard of personal presentation: immaculate appearance, up to date without being over-trendy, discreet make-up, good haircut.
- Commitment to client service: fully support that the client comes first and that they can feel exposed and vulnerable when receiving treatments.
- Selling skills: able to offer clients/customers additional products and services appropriate to their needs without over-persuading. Have acquired many repeat clients in my most recent job.
- Discretion: special skills in intimate waxing; able to deal with potentially embarrassing conditions sympathetically and professionally; able to use hot (hard) wax safely and effectively with excellent results.
- Pigmentation disorders: completed BeautyFirst course in pigmentation disorders including 'camouflage' treatments for severe conditions. Have worked as volunteer for local branch of Changing Faces, charity devoted to the needs of people with severe facial disfigurements.
- Advanced eyelash extension skills.
- Manicure and pedicure skills.
- Wedding and other special occasions make-up; have now created make-up for 8 brides and their mothers/bridesmaids.
- Trained by Foreman-Stanton in colour and style analysis, so able to advise clients on colours and styles that suit them along with the right styles and colours of make-up.

*CAREER HISTORY*

2010–present
Freelance beauty therapist, working on contract at Gayles' Spa, Esporta and Fitness Express Gym and with my own clients.

2009–10
Studying for my NVQ; supported self with variety of freelance and casual work including beauty therapy, Royal Mail, shop assistant at Freeman's, delivering pamphlets, bar work.

2008–9
Receptionist, Frizell's Printing: carried out all reception duties, e.g. welcomed and looked after visitors, managed security arrangements, made tea and coffee, took messages, kept reception area immaculate, arranged flowers and managed switchboard, often under time pressure; being organized and friendly at all times was key to success in the role

2007–8
Salon assistant, Grant Samson. Assisted with hair-washing, kept salon clean and tidy; learnt hair colour techniques, manicure and facial skills under supervision of experienced stylist and beauty therapist.

2005–6
Shop assistant, River Island.

2000–5
Self-employed. Variety of short-term contracts, freelance work, temping including office assistant, filing clerk, selling franchised perfume, dancer, mini-cabbing.

*EDUCATION*

2010 Exeter College. Beauty Therapy NVQ Level 2, distinctions

2008 Foreman-Stanton: Colour and Style course

2011 BeautyFirst: Pigmentation Disorders course

2000 Grebe School: A levels in Geography and Media Studies; GCSEs in English, Maths, Geography, History, Science

*PERSONAL INTERESTS*
All aspects of fashion and style; travelling with friends; garage music, dancing.

# Young professional seeking a change of firm

Sheena has been with the same firm of actuaries since leaving university. It has been enjoyable and she has done well. Her firm is about to be merged with a competitor. This could be good for an ambitious young professional because it could create many new opportunities for further advancement and there is no pressure on her to leave. But Sheena has privately decided that this might be a good time to move on and intends to contact a few headhunters with a view to joining a company with an internationally based business.

The CV challenge for anyone working in a professional services firm (for instance, accountancy, the law, management consultancy) is to demonstrate that you really have made a difference rather than just doing your job. The more your service is about giving advice rooted in a complex subject such as the law, the more nebulous it can seem and the greater the temptation just to make your CV a faint echo of your job description, especially as in the early years of such careers you are essentially building your experience while you follow in the shadow of a much more experienced principal. In many such professions, the work is actually about long-term trends and slow changes, many of which may be imperceptible at the time. Despite this, Sheena has been able to make some impressive claims about her record and to demonstrate the skills and knowledge she would bring to a new job. She has chosen the chronological format as it seems the most straightforward in her case.

---

Page 1 of 2

**Sheena Howerd-Leggett, FIA**
Tyrone House, Old Broadway, Manchester M20
09876 7756432     email S.Howerd.Leggett@aol.com

### PROFILE

Confident, outgoing and ambitious consulting actuary with strong communication and consulting skills and 11 years' experience in pensions and liability management. A long-term thinker with a flair for creativity and innovation.

### CAREER HISTORY

September 2006 to date

**Fine & Silkins Ltd, Manchester,** *Corporate pensions consulting actuary*
Leading a client portfolio of six companies with pension schemes varying from under £100m to over £10bn.

> *Long-term thinking:* advise clients on 20–30-year implications of their current pension dilemmas, working closely with CEOs and CFOs of FTSE organizations and their boards.

> *Managing down pension costs:* have worked closely with clients on pension benefits, reducing costs by 10–20%, reflected in eventual P&L results; advised on methods of avoiding increases, keeping costs steady for two client organizations despite volatility of the last two years.

> *Restructuring investments:* advised clients successfully on improved approaches to match assets to liabilities.

*Benefit reviews:* developed innumerable creative approaches to client schemes which have enabled them to redesign pension schemes where, for example, inflation-proof pensions have been exchanged for higher initial payments.

*Consulting skills:* create close, mutually trustful relationships with clients, enabling both challenge and support to be part of the way we work together.

*Multinational working:* developed approaches to help clients ameliorate and understand differences made by pension traditions and legislation in different countries.

*Communication:* have developed effective ways of demystifying complex data to clients, explaining in simple terms without losing the integrity of the ideas. Have also worked with client communication specialists in one organization, developing strategies for anticipating and overcoming member resistance to changes in pension schemes, for instance designing a series of workshops delivered across UK and Europe.

*Business development:* worked closely with sales team to provide input to proposals for prospective clients; headed up the technical aspects of the presentation, resulting in winning business from two substantial new clients.

*'Thought leadership':* lead the UK group of liability management specialists, calling regular meetings to brainstorm new approaches, tools and techniques. Group has developed many successful ideas which have been converted into standard practice across the firm.

*Coaching and mentoring:* act as formal mentor to 3 actuarial students; informally offer mentoring to colleagues across the UK branches.

*Conference speaking:* regular contributor to national and international conferences on liability management topics.

### 2004–2006
Consultant
Worked as a consulting actuary supporting principals on delivery of work; developed specialism in liability management issues during this time.

### 1999–2004
Actuarial student
Worked in the pensions consulting department working on both company and trustee work. Carried out the usual mix of student work: calculations, accounting and valuations.

## EDUCATION AND QUALIFICATIONS
Institute of Actuaries: FIA 2003
1996 to 1999: University of Warwick; BSc (Hons) Mathematics 2:1

## INTERESTS
Squash, tennis, skiing, fell walking, Italian cooking.

A further 14 example CVs are available on the Kogan Page website. To access, go to http://www.koganpage.com/editions/great-answers-to-tough-cv-problems/9780749462802

With over 1,000 titles in printed and digital format, **Kogan Page** offers affordable, sound business advice

**www.koganpage.com**

With over 42 years of publishing, more than 80 million people have succeeded in business with thanks to **Kogan Page**

**www.koganpage.com**